MOVE AHEAD!

"Once you have used possibility thinking to create a peaceful mind; once you have learned the true way to meditate and pray; you will have removed the negative tensions that block creative impulses, that stifle the enjoyment of life, that prevent the achievement of goals. You will be able to move ahead to the life God wants you to have."
—Robert H. Schuller

ROBERT H. SCHULLER

PEACE OF MIND THROUGH POSSIBILITY THINKING

A JOVE BOOK

This Jove book contains the complete
text of the original hardcover edition.
It has been completely reset in a typeface
designed for easy reading and was printed
from new film.

PEACE OF MIND THROUGH POSSIBILITY THINKING

A Jove Book / published by arrangement with
Doubleday & Company, Inc.

PRINTING HISTORY
Doubleday & Company edition published 1977
Jove edition / November 1978
Fourteenth printing / July 1986

ISBN: 0-515-08985-0

Library of Congress Catalog Card Number: 72-76203

Jove Books are published by The Berkley Publishing Group,
200 Madison Avenue, New York, N.Y. 10016.
The words "A JOVE BOOK" and the "J" with sunburst
are trademarks belonging to Jove Publications, Inc.

PRINTED IN THE UNITED STATES OF AMERICA

Contents

PEACE
OF MIND
THROUGH
POSSIBILITY
THINKING

Introduction

The night is calm. The sea is gentle. The tropical breeze is stirring in the palm garden below my balcony, a half moon is reflected on the shimmering ripples of a quiet and peaceful Atlantic Ocean that surrounds this strong and invincible volcanic island called Madeira. In a few hours the sun will rise over the jagged, rugged mountains, jungle green with lush banana groves. And my nameless canary will start singing again. She's just a little bird. So small. She lives and spends every day in the glorious tropical paradise of swaying palms, blossoming cactus outside our room here at the famous Reids Hotel.

I checked into this room with Mrs. Schuller to complete the writing of this book. I knew I needed protection from unwelcome, pressure-producing, tension-generating interruptions if I was to be creative.

Tension seems to be our constant companion in this stress-torn world. The inner calm that is our birthright is continuously assailed by noise, pollution, inflation, illness, personal problems involving children and parents, and a myriad of other debilitating experiences including even the threat of annihilation. The tension produced in our mind and spirit often results in mental and physical illness and the inability to effectively achieve our life goals.

In this book I will show you the way to eliminate tension from your life and replace it with peace of mind, achieved through possibility thinking. Those who have read my previous books, especially *Move Ahead with Possibility Thinking,* know the tenets of possibility thinking and what a possibility thinker is.

A possibility thinker is a person who, when faced with a mountain does not quit. He keeps on striving until he climbs over, finds a pass through, tunnels underneath, or simply stays, and turns his mountain into a gold mine with God's help. A possibility thinker looks for all the possibilities in every situation instead of the impossibilities.

A possibility thinker overcomes feelings of inadequacy and replaces them with self-confidence. He is open to new ideas and new ways of doing things. He learns to recognize opportunities and does something about them. He looks at problems as challenges to be met and solved. He faces personal tragedies with faith and a peaceful mind.

I will show you, by using possibility thinking, how to turn tension into creative channels. You will learn how to derive great power from your new peace-centered mind. Once you have learned the secret of tranquillity and serenity, you will be able to forge a joyous, abundant, fulfilled and productive existence.

It is not coincidental that the rise of tension as an emotional epidemic parallels continuing reports of the lack of communication between persons. One reason for lack of communication is that inner tension blocks the mind from hearing what others are really saying. It also blocks the mind from hearing what God is saying.

In this book you will discover a profound principle: *Tranquillity is conditioning for communication.*

Once, when I was a young man, I had a strange, beautiful, transcendent experience with "God" in the mountains. But then I came back to civilization, to the "real world." And suddenly, the "religious feeling" was gone and I suspected, therefore, the integrity of it. "I was manipulated by the idyllic setting," I falsely reasoned. I crudely concluded that the world of traffic and crowds was "reality," the peaceful world of the silent hills was "unreality."

Years later, my thinking would be straightened out, quite indirectly, by the sound theology and psychology (though he never realized that's what it was) of architect Richard Neutra. Neutra was to become a profound influence in my life in teaching me "bio-realism."

The truth is that our Creator has, like a brilliant cosmic architect, designed an incredible organism called "Human Being." In His basic planning God conceived of engineering with this person a built-in tranquillizing system so relaxed and at peace, that every person would be sensitive and receptive to receive daily spiritual communication from the Creator.

Communication is, of course, the placing of a positive suggestion in a suggestible or deeply relaxed mind. So, according to Neutra's "bio-realism," God created us with eyes to see clouds sliding silently through the soundless sea of space, and green trees bending gently in soft breezes; water shimmering in the moonlight. Seeing the scene of serenity, Man and Woman would enjoy deep calm and Quiet Inner Peace. They would be ready to hear that "still small inner voice of God" who planned for birds to fly, fish to swim, and persons to walk in gardens. Sounds too! God planned ears to hear tranquil sounds. The rustle of the wind. The song of the bird. The trickle of a friendly brook. More peace! Deeper relaxation, heightened sensitivity to the sounds of the Spirit!

But a terrible thing happened. There was a first battle in a first garden and there was fighting. In despera-

11

tion the Man and his Woman left the natural habitat.

Today, we have left the garden far behind. The ears and the eyes, designed to be channels of tranquillity, have become loud corridors where a mad assortment of tensions rage and race in wild abandon.

The biological organism is having a problem. And beyond that—the Spirit that dwells in the biological organism is the first to feel the sickening shock. No longer does God's message come through with simplicity. The static of many tensions jams the spiritual wave lengths. Adam and Eve are out of their garden!

The human being is in an ecologically, psychologically, and spiritually polluted environment when he leaves his natural Garden of Eden and is thrown into a foreign jungle of cars, buses, concrete, and asphalt. Few cold, calculating, logical atheists have realized that their unbelief is the negative emotional reaction of an organism that is intellectually and emotionally confused because it is out of its natural habitat.

To tranquillize is to condition for communication. So, Neutra taught me: "When I design your church it will be planned so close to nature that we will give the Creator a chance to use the built-in tranquilizing system again. We shall block out the ugly power line with solid walls; we shall throw open windows to the big sky! We shall bring the gentle sound of water into the place of peace. Tranquillized, relaxed, we shall be receptive to the natural flow of God's creative thoughts."

Architecture will come to the rescue of theology and psychology!

The result? I have lived and worked in that structure for nearly twenty years now. I have seen over seven thousand secular, spiritually insensitive persons become whole and healthy believers in that place.

Dr. René Dubos said it in words to this effect:

"What I fear is man's ability to adjust." By that he meant that human beings inherit an evolutionary capacity to adjust and adjust downward to survive in an alien, hostile, destructive environment. Why fear that? Because we will one day be born breathing unclean air, drinking impure water, listening to tension-producing sounds, and, unaware, we will not care that we are destroying ourselves, spiritually and emotionally, in the adjusting process.

So under the steadily mounting stress and strain that naturally afflicts any organism that is out of its natural habitat, man—an intrinsically and incurably spiritual creature—has become sick with a tension-induced sickness called "secularism." "God is dead!" he shouts.

Whom are we to believe? The secularist who says, "There is no God"? Or the religious person who declares, "I know God is alive—I experience Him"? I was asked that question recently by a leading secular radio commentator who was interviewing me in Hong Kong. My answer? "If a bird that has spent all its life in a cage declares, 'I do not believe in the sky! I do not believe in soaring—it's impossible!' I would not believe that bird! If a fish that has been living all of its wet life in a fish bowl denies belief in the lakes, streams, and seas, I would not believe that fish. If a person who has spent his life in an environment of cars, streets, curbs, concrete, and asphalt, breathing exhaust—pushed, shoved, elbowed, and dehumanized by his own species and depersonalized by a computerized, technological, materialistic world—if such a person says, 'I don't believe in God'—I would not trust his judgment!"

A bird was designed to fly; a fish to swim; and persons to enjoy God in a garden. Gardens tranquillize. And tranquillity makes spiritual communication possible.

13

As you learn in this book to relax and achieve mental tranquillity, you will find yourself being receptive to creative ideas. You will also discover that God is communicating with you.

Once you have used possibility thinking to create a peaceful mind; once you have learned the true way to meditate and to pray; you will have removed the negative tensions that block creative impulses, that stifle the enjoyment of life, that prevent the achievement of goals. You will be able to move ahead to the life God wants you to have.

Read on—discover how to achieve inner tranquillity, peace of mind through possibility thinking. And amazing power will unfold in your life.

Robert Schuller

Madeira
July 19, 1977

PEACE
OF MIND
THROUGH
POSSIBILITY
THINKING

I

The Power of a Tranquil Mind

How would you describe your life in emotional terms?

Are you happy-go-lucky? Or uptight and tense?

Do you feel pleasantly relaxed or squeezed by many pressures?

Do you go to work on Monday cheerful and optimistic or gloomy and fatigued?

Do you find your enthusiasm turning into despondency?

Are you seldom really joyful—but more often grimly satisfied or gravely anxious?

Do you find negative emotions and upsetting and unsettling thoughts dominating your mind most of the time?

Is your life today less than satisfying and do you often feel mysteriously unhappy?

If so, you may be living with enthusiasm-draining, mind-confusing, life-restricting tension. You may be one of those millions of people who have let tension take over your life. You may be one of those who are being kept from having a fruitful, stimulating, wonderful, happy life because tension is dominating your inner self.

It is only when a tension-tortured person replaces inner turmoil with a quiet, peaceful and harmonious center that innate powers are released. Then it becomes possible to realize dreams, to think creatively, to reach exciting goals—to live—and to live joyously.

You Will Learn to Relax—Naturally.

Unfortunately, we seem to live in a tension-filled world. If you analyze this one particular aspect of our existence, you'll find it to be a major deterrent to a functioning, happy life. Tension goes under many names. It is often called stress. Or, sometimes, pressure. In its more advanced stages it becomes anxiety. Then there is the relatively new word—uptight. The Merriam-Webster Dictionary defines uptight as "being tense, nervous, or uneasy."

The word "tension" leaps at us from the pages of newspapers and magazines and from our television screens. Commercials offer a variety of tension-easing pills and nostrums promising instant release and relief from the headaches, backaches, and stomach aches caused by nervous pressure. Just think—twenty million sleeping pills are swallowed every night in the United States alone. Twelve million pounds of aspirin are consumed every year. And 250 million tranquillizers like Valium and Librium and others are prescribed and used each year.

For what purpose? To what end?

To ease tension.

Yet all of these, even if taken together, cannot accomplish in reality the one thing they are supposed to do. At best, they are impermanent, giving a few moments or hours of relief from the symptoms of tension.

Tension and its attendant symptoms cannot be dissolved by a pill. Its roots lie deep in the human spirit. Discover that "still power" that is greater than "pill power." Uncover, eliminate, and replace your tensions with peace of mind. "Be still and know I am God."

You Will Experience Expanded Awareness.

Have you ever noticed when you return from a vacation trip that your house or apartment looks different? It hasn't changed. You have.

Before your trip you had become so used to the colors, textures, and the arrangement of your furniture that they seemed almost not to be there. You were so distracted and occupied by the tensions of daily life that these tensions slowly and imperceptibly clouded the windows of your awareness center. When you went on vacation you began to relax and put the cares, stresses, and strains of your existence to one side. By the time of your return the fogged-up windows of your inner awareness had begun to clear. As you entered your home you saw your possessions with a new clear-eyed vision and an unclouded inner awareness.

As you develop peace of mind, many ordinary things will begin to look different to you. You will be inspired with flashing facets of life that you never suspected existed. Your perception of the world around you will be sharpened astonishingly. You will "become religious" when you haven't been. Unnatural, anti-human tension restricts a person's normal sensitivity to the reality of God. That explains why many people feel closer to God in nature, and conversely, why an increasingly tension-filled world is become more secular.

Religious unbelief is a condition in the human being and is always the result of a surface, or an exceedingly deep-seated, tension that blocks normal, health-producing faith.

Religious unbelief is one result of unhealthy tensions

produced by our emotional reaction to an ecologically imbalanced life style.

You Will Raise Your Consciousness Level.

There is much said and written today about consciousness raising. People everywhere talk about the various ways of raising their consciousness to achieve new awareness.

Unfortunately, many tens of thousands of young people (and some older, also) have turned to drugs to achieve this purpose. Drugs give an unreal and false sense of heightened awareness. And since it isn't real, it doesn't last. When it's over drug users come thumping back to earth, back to dull reality from which they've been trying to escape. Often they are scarred and maimed by the effects of the drugs they've taken.

Just as all the aspirin, sleeping pills, tranquillizers, and other chemicals either professionally prescribed or bought over the counter cannot bring permanent release from tension or anxiety, neither can drugs—whether marijuana, LSD, heroin, cocaine, or alcohol. Nor does any change of consciousness they might briefly bring do anything to develop a true peace-centered mind. A true peace-centered mind is needed if the power for a successful and rewarding life is to be obtained. All the nostrums and false means of eliminating tensions and raising your sights are as nothing compared to the vast power of Possibility Thinking which I share with you in this book. For Possibility Thinking is the key to an exciting, authentic "religious experience."

It is a common experience for new converts to Christianity to say that on the following morning the entire world looked so beautiful. In conversion, the tension

created by guilt, loneliness, alienation, and meaninglessness in life is eliminated, and deep peace of mind comes
over the person as a result of the experience of salvation.

Suddenly, he sees with a new and expanded awareness—

—the flowers that had been blooming for days in the
garden

—the birds sitting, singing and flying. His ears hear
with greater clarity—

—the whisper of the wind in the treetops

—the chirping of the crickets in the garden

—the laughter of children at play

—the chatter of birds

Indeed, all of nature's sounds and sights become
clearer, more understandable and more pleasurable.

You Will Tap a Powerful Source of Creativity.

As your perception and consciousness are heightened
you are coming close to contacting an incredible and
exciting source of creativity. Relaxation focuses the
screen of your inner-mind on a sharp creativity.

My office is in the Tower of Hope, a fourteen-story
structure on the grounds of the Garden Grove Community Church. I have come to realize that when I am in
my office I am seldom able to be really creative. I don't
seem to be able to relax completely. At any moment my
secretary may buzz me on the intercom to announce a
visitor or ask a question. There is always a list of necessary phone calls to make and the returning of calls I
couldn't answer before. I am probably very aware of a
forthcoming meeting for which I must prepare or a visit
that must be made before the day is over. So you see,

21

even the routine events of everyday life produce tension. It is possible even for small tensions to constrict, choke, and clog the channels through which positive and creative ideas flow. A dead spider in the thermostat in our church once turned off the entire air conditioning system.

In order to relax completely so as to become creative, I find I must be in a place where I am protected from tension-producing interruptions, which explains why creative solutions to problems often come in the middle of the night. A mind clogged with the pressures of everyday living or with a major problem cannot think clearly, creatively, or constructively.

My creative spurts come when I am driving my car or I am away for a few days in a mountain retreat where no doorbells or telephones can interrupt the flow of ideas. Often my most creative thoughts come to mind when I am alone in a hotel room in a strange city or running alone in my morning exercises. At times like these I can be alone with my God, who is your God, too. Creativity takes place when I know, at the deepest level, that I am in tune with Him and the two of us are protected from unexpected and unwelcomed interruptions.

Sheltered in my solitude from tension-producing interruptions, I find I must first clear my mind of the debris of the problems and tensions that may have built up in the previous hours, days, or weeks. This I can do by repeating a favorite Bible verse. Perhaps the Twenty-third Psalm, whose very words, when repeated, bring forth a wave of cool, calming peace which covers the soul and mind with serenity and quietude:

The Lord is my shepherd; I shall not want.
He makes me lie down in green pastures;

He leads me beside the still waters,
He restores my soul; . . .

Following this a deep feeling of peace overtakes me.
After ten to twenty minutes of this quietude, I feel a
mysterious strength being aroused and arising within me
the ability to think positively, creatively, and power-
fully. New ideas leap into my mind. Solutions to problems form in a logical way. I see clearly into the future
and make decisions as to necessary courses of action.

Christians have always used meditation as a way of
opening the door to solutions of life's problems. Meditation has always been an important adjunct to the practice of Christianity. Through the ages, monks in monasteries have spent endless hours in prayer and
meditation. In a relaxed state of mind, they made contact with the Source of All Creativity, and ideas began
to flow.

New ideas, positive solutions to problems, and direction in decision making will come to you also through
Peace of Mind living.

You Will Maintain Vital Energy.

The Possibility Thinking, peaceful mind generates
creative ideas which produce enthusiasm which *is* energy! So the Possibility Thinking peace-centered mind
is constantly and enthusiastically planning, creating, and
producing ideas which stimulate boundless energy to
achieve incredible goals.

You will literally experience a new and abundant life
when you learn to:

23

Turn Energy-producing Power On.
Turn Fatigue-producing Tension Off.

Nothing can tire you faster than stress and strain. How many times have you heard people say, "I'm just not up to it," or, "I'm too tired now, I'll finish it tomorrow." They are probably victims of energy-draining tension.

While on a visit to Fuju, Japan, some years ago, I was given a tour and briefed on the activities of the entire Asian Communications Center of the United States military forces. In the weather section the chief called me over to a radio-controlled photographic transmitting machine and asked me to watch what was being received.

I watched a photograph unroll from the machine. When completed it looked as if a photo had been taken of a giant spinning top. The chief's face was tense as he said, "That's a typhoon. It's heading straight for the Philippines. Tomorrow it'll hit and hit hard."

Then he pointed to a white dot in the center of the picture and said, "There's the famous quiet-power center."

All of the power within typhoons—that power which develops winds up to 190 miles an hour—originates in the calm "eye" or center of the phenomenon. The violent tornadoes or cyclones on land and the furious hurricanes of the North Atlantic also have a quiet, peaceful center.

I want you to learn the secret of achieving your own quiet-power from a peace-centered mind. Then, someday, if it were possible to take a photograph of your inner being we would see a silver center of serenity. Achieve this inner calmness of soul, and instead of destructive emotional storms, a fresh, youthful, energizing power will well up within you! You will be driven by a controlled force that will produce constructive, creative thinking and action.

Human energy does not originate in the muscles. Energy is generated in the psyche or spirit, that certain being contained within all of God's people. Just as the quiet-power center of the typhoon is at the heart of tremendous and violent action, so the peace-centered mind generates the psychic energy which is then transformed into physical and mental activity. You'll find that you will be able to maintain vital energy and overcome emotional fatigue after you achieve that glorious peace of mind.

It is important to make a distinction between exhaustion and fatigue. Exhaustion is that relatively brief, "I've got to sit down a minute" feeling that you get after strenuous, maximum physical effort. It is often accompanied by a pleasant sensation of proud accomplishment. Usually after a short rest you are ready to go on to the next task.

Fatigue, long-lasting and continuous, is caused by emotional tension that assaults the organism. Fatigue is a weariness of the body that reflects a weariness of the soul. If inner tension is combined with physical exertion, you will not be exhausted, you'll be fatigued.

Often you need not even exert yourself to feel fatigue; you're fatigued before you move one muscle. I'm sure you've known people who complain of being tired as soon as they arise in the morning. Sometimes it has a physical cause. However, if a person is unable to deflect tension, his body will reflect tension in emotional fatigue.

I promise that I can show you a way to turn your tensions off and develop peace of mind deep within yourself. When you have learned how to have a peace-centered mind, you will find a new life of youthful power and energy. Surely, steadily, smoothly, and serenely, as you turn your tensions off and replace them with a peace-centered mind, you will find the power, a dynamic source of energy that will help you overcome your difficulties and move you forward to meet your goals.

You Will Live a Longer, Healthier Life.

It's understandable then that, with a peace-centered mind you will live a longer and happier life. Most medical experts agree that tension is a top-ranking enemy of good health. Tension might well be called the number one killer itself, as it leads to hypertension, alcoholism, heart disease, ulcers, intestinal disorders, to mention only a few of the disabling and killing maladies.

The word disease is made up of two syllables—*dis* and *ease*. Dis-ease is lack of ease. When you are ill at ease, you are tense. So, you see there is even a philological relationship between tension and disease.

It therefore follows that when you rid yourself of tension and replace it with a peace-centered mind, it will mean a healthier, longer, and happier life for you.

You Will Live a Happier Life.

Yes, you'll really start enjoying life—not just enduring it. Love, laughter, affection, humor, enthusiasm, and joy are warm, positive emotions. Icy tension freezes over to trap these emotions under a cold cap of ice as surely as a deep winter freeze forms an ice layer over the pleasant waters of a lovely lake.

At the same time that tension is freezing these positive emotions, it is releasing a chilling mental climate of negative emotions—fear, anger, boredom, and jealousy.

The divine Peace that will come into your heart and into the control center of your mind will thaw the icy tension. Just as the warm spring sun thaws the winter ice and turns cold water warm, so will positive emotions be released and replace the negative, frigid feelings.

Like springtime after winter, a balmy optimism, cheerful expectations, and a hopeful mental outlook will thaw out your fears, apprehensions, and anxieties. At first a trickle, then a stream of tension-producing negative emotions drain out of your mind, leaving your consciousness like warm spring soil—fertile and receptive for fruitful seed-planting.

You'll find yourself looking forward to a knock on the door or a ring of the doorbell, the telephone call from a friend or relative, exciting news in a letter in the mailbox. By now your life is really being transformed at a very deep level.

You Will Develop Improved Communication Skills.

There is one wonderful principle that you will detect weaving its way through this book. Look for it. Understand it.

Here it is: *tranquillity is conditioning for creative communication*. So peace of mind (tranquillity) prepares you, at the deepest level of your being (conditions you) to be a practitioner of Possibility Thinking (creative communication).

Am I saying that some persons who are negative thinkers (practice impossibility thinking) become incapable of being possibility thinkers while they are tense? Yes.

Many who read my first book, *Move Ahead with Possibility Thinking,* failed to find help because they never developed into possibility thinkers. Why didn't they? Perhaps it was because the theme and the truth of the book were too threatening to them! (Which is another way of saying that inner tensions kept them from relaxing enough to absorb what we were trying to say.)

If I now say that peace of mind produces Possibility Thinking is this different from saying that Possibility Thinking produces peace of mind? Which is truer? Neither, and both. It's like asking, What comes first, the chicken or the egg? What starts effective communication—hearing or speaking? Talking or listening?

You can become an effective communicator when you learn to listen to new ideas. You'll start listening when you relax, and reduce your tensions and tensions in those to whom you wish to relate. Disentangle yourself from those inner tensions that produce locked-in thinking and you will begin to listen to truths that you were either: (a) Too defensive to deeply and honestly hear; (b) too afraid to even try to understand.

In any and all interpersonal relationships there is a vast variety of verbalized and non-verbalized threats, real and imaginary, that can—and will—produce enough tensions to prevent life changing, situation altering, communication.

The thought of changing one's mind is a threat to insecure people. So only deeply secure (self-loving) persons dare (are relaxed enough) to really listen.

I sensed this at one of the International Congresses of Psychologists. The Soviet psychologists did not really hear what the psychologists from the free world were saying. While we were studying behavior modification

28

(how do you change people) there was a discussion on "the ethics of Behavior Modification." Do we have the ethical freedom to manipulate? Brainwash? To create threats, which become a conditioned stimuli, to produce a modification or change in behavior—for the purpose of converting people to our side and then controlling them so we can maintain or enlarge our personal power base? This is one of the great questions of our time.

In truth, relaxation is essential before there can be constructive dialogue. And when peace of mind improves your communication then amazingly, even old walls of resentment start falling down.

You Will Notice Your Interpersonal Relationships Improving.

Obviously, if communication improves between you and those around you, your relationships will be amazingly transformed for the better. We need not belabor the obvious—that problems in interpersonal relationships (between husband and wife, parent and child, employer and employee) are the result of barriers to, or breakdowns in communication.

What you will achieve—perhaps indirectly rather than directly—out of this book, is a real development in your relationships.

Marriages will improve; other ruptured relationships will begin to repair themselves.

Tense people don't dare to listen for fear that they might agree with the other person, which could be costly. They might have to change their minds, their ways, even their jobs or their religion (or lack of it).

Insecure people find the prospect of changing their minds a challenge to a basically weak ego.

Can you imagine how threatening it would be to change your life or your thoughts if it meant severing you from what might be a major source of your ego fulfillment? This explains why a professional atheist I know is super-tense, and barring a miracle of God's grace (and I believe in miracles) is condemned all her days to hold to her professional atheism. This, after all, is her "ego trip." Tension, of course, is often a defense mechanism and maneuver that we use to manipulate ourselves to avoid encountering the threat of a truth that would convert or change us. It might force us to find new and necessary sources of nourishment to strengthen our egos, or face emotional deprivation, if not starvation!

An intellectual who was an atheist visited our church in Garden Grove "to see the architecture." Because there were few religious symbols there—mostly sky, grass and trees, he didn't feel threatened, so he relaxed. This deep relaxation made him receptive to really "listen" to the forceful truth of love. He felt a "presence within" and yielded to it. Now he is an emotionally healthy believer healed of his neurotic unbelief. He is an active worker on our twenty-four-hour telephone counseling suicide-prevention program.

"It makes me feel good to know that God is using me to help lost people find the way," he has said, adding, "that good feeling is a really satisfying and safe supply for my ego needs. To think I used to feed my ego with my masterful negative intellectualizations."

You can see now, how Possibility Thinking (creative listening) and peace of mind (deep relaxation) go hand in hand with (a) communication which leads to (b) new and improved relationships (c) making you a healthier and happier all around person to be with.

30

Truly—nothing is more important than peace of mind.

Read on and you'll find this pearl of great price! Your life will be so transformed you'll literally "be born again."

II

Self-love—The Silent Spring of Serenity

The destructive assortment of negative tensions that rob us of peace of mind are many and far-reaching like the branches of a banyan tree. However, the tap root of that tree out of which all negative tensions spring is a lack of self-esteem or a negative self-image.

If you denigrate yourself, belittle your God-given abilities, and negatively say to yourself, "I can't do it"; "I'm no good"; then you have an inadequate self-image and you can be sure this will produce an unbelievable assortment of troubles for your mind as well as your body.

Modern medicine along with modern psychology agrees with modern theology that loving oneself rightly is an essential prelude to living a full, happy, and fruitful existence.

If you lack a strong sense of self-regard, it is all-important that you develop one. Cut the tap root of a tree and watch the leaves wither and the unripened fruit fall. Learn to love yourself and you'll find a vast variety of tensions dissolving like fog in the morning sun. With growing self-assurance, you will go on to experience an emerging peace-centered and creative mind.

The truth is that every human being has problems with his self-image. We are all born with a negative self-image. The Bible tells us the story of Adam who was created clean and perfect. Like the child of a famous father who may be tempted to rebel against his father's overpowering shadow, perhaps Adam was tempted to assert himself and sin. When that happened, he became separated from God. Feeling guilty, he hid in the bushes to avoid being caught by the Almighty. Since Adam, all human beings are "born in the bushes." That is what "original sin" is all about. It means we are all born detached from a relationship with God, and consequently suffer from birth with a terribly weak and insecure ego. That's another way of saying we're all born with a negative self-image. This indeed is the core of "sin."

This alienation from God deprives us of the self-assurance, self-affirmation, self-confidence generating relationship with Him, which leaves us so emotionally starved that we become vain, rebellious and self-serving, all because at the outset of our lives we are born with an inadequate self-love.

Erik Erikson's studies of the stages of child development throw light on this concept. Dr. Erikson, the "father of child psychiatry," tells us an infant is born untrusting. The point is profoundly theological—we are all born with a negative self-image. Somehow we must be born again and emerge trusting and enthused about the kind of persons we can be with the help of God.

What Is Self-love?

Some people upon hearing the words *self-love* misinterpret its meaning. Self-love is not narcissism, vanity, or self-admiration. It is not being enamored or entranced with your personal appearance.

Self-love is not self-glorification. It is not the continu-

34

ous attempt to impress others with your importance, with the position you occupy or the awards and accolades won.

Self-love is not being arrogant or snobbish. It is not the condescending attitude you have when you feel you are superior to other persons. It *is* loving others as yourself no matter what their origins, background, race, or religion.

Self-love is not self-will. Self-will is actually the defensive, and even potentially dangerous and demonic behavior of an insecure, non-self-loving person. Even as self-love is the tap root of peace of mind, so self-will is the polluting source of destructive tensions.

Self-will is that raw, rough, inconsiderate selfishness that takes the attitude, "I want what I want when I want it." Self-will is that rigid, unyielding, stubborn spirit of a person who, at his deepest level, is too insecure to ever compromise; too lacking in self-love to generously share himself; too void of self-assurance to ever publicly admit that he made a mistake. A stubborn self-will is the tension-generating behavior of a deeply insecure person. What a tragic cycle of tensions is set in motion. A mental climate of antagonism, hostility, resentment, jealousy, and frustration is produced. All of this, of course, produces new tensions and troubles for the self-willed person, and each new tension only seeks to reinforce and harden his desperate, defensive, and insecure behavior. He's caught in an ever-widening whirlpool of tensions!

What, then, is self-love?

Basically, self-love embodies respect for yourself; what the ancient Greeks called, "reverence for the self." This is expressed in a number of different ways.

In the Bible there is the classic section known as "the

love chapter." Put the word "self" in front of the word love and you'll read:

> Self-love is patient and kind.
> Self-love is not jealous or boastful.
> Self-love is not arrogant or rude.
> It does not insist on its own way.

Self-love is a healthy pride. It is being proud of who you are. Without self-love, many people are ashamed of their ancestry or their humble beginnings. They look with awe on those who boast of their descent from European nobility, or from the Mayflower settlers of the Massachusetts Bay Colony. "I feel I have royal blood in my veins," a black friend said to me, adding with ennobling self-respect, "I may or may not have the blood of an African chief in my heart, but I do know I am descended from some of the earliest settlers of this country. And my ancestors, though slaves, worked sacrificially to help make this country what it is today." No matter what nation your predecessors came from, there is and was a culture in that place unlike any other in the world.

The famous English Prime Minister Benjamin Disraeli was once taunted by a political opponent for being a Jew. He replied, "Yes, I am a Jew and when the ancestors of the right honorable gentlemen were brutal savages on an unknown island, mine were priests in the Temple of Solomon."

The self-loving person also develops and expresses a very healthy self-confidence. The lack of self-confidence is one of the major roadblocks to peace of mind, happiness, and success in life. For self-confidence is the belief in your own ability to come to grips with problems and solve them; to know that you can and will succeed at worthy tasks; all of which equips you emotionally to meet life's challenges with equanimity and imperturbability.

The self-confident person, in turn, dares to be an honest, open person. He accepts himself as a unique individual. He reflects a basic integrity of character.

He becomes genuinely and infectiously enthusiastic. Only honest persons can be enthusiastic. Insecure persons keep their little dark secrets locked and hopefully hidden from public view. So they develop a tense, psychic, invisible emotional barrier that constantly restrains their inclination to be enthusiastic. This is an acquired defense mechanism designed to keep oneself from "talking too much" and "letting the cat out of the bag," and exposing one's true and blacker self. Honest persons, by contrast, are truly free. They are naturally enthusiastic because they have nothing to hide.

The person who is enthusiastic about himself, in turn, is self-assured and relaxed. He finds it easy to give in, back down, admit his errors, and change his mind when new light is shed. Instead of being defensive, he dares to seek constructive criticism. "Do you see any problems in my plan?" "Do you see how I can improve my work?" "Can you offer any suggestions?" are the questions of a self-loving person. This self-assured behavior sets a dynamic cycle in motion. That person creates a mental climate of trust, respect, affection. People start treating him beautifully. They really do help him with creative criticism which reduces his mistakes, boosts his achievements and strengthens his relationships, all of which reinforces his self-respect. He starts a fantastic peace-of-mind cycle. For he relaxes tension around him producing peace in his life and in the lives of others. He's on the way!

You can see, now, that self-love is indeed the core to

a genuinely peace-centered mind. As you use the principles below to build a strong self-love, you will, in the process, be strengthening other positive personality traits. These include self-discovery, self-discipline, self-development, and self-dedication. All of which adds up to achieving responsible personhood—both the end and the means of peace of mind.

You will also find vast areas of untapped resources within yourself when you start relaxing. Just as the seemingly barren deserts produce amazing quantities of oil and the bare rugged mountains, seemingly worthless, contain valuable mineral deposits, so there are mental and spiritual resources hidden deep within your mind and spirit waiting to be discovered and uncovered.

Listen to the words of Jesus Christ in the Sermon on the Mount:

> You are the salt of the earth.
> You are the light of the world.

He was telling all of us—"You are somebody and don't be afraid to believe in yourself—bring forth your talents and really try to become all you were meant to be."

Last, and far from least, when you develop a positive self-image, you'll know that God can live—and move and have His being within you. When you experience God in your consciousness, you will believe even more strongly in His still small voice within you. This, then, will tremendously boost your growing self-confidence!

Eleven Steps to Building a Strong Self-love.

You can succeed now in becoming a strong character. Self-assured! Secure! Confident! Relaxed! Here's how:

1. *Learn how to handle competition creatively.* Perhaps nothing robs our minds of peace and leaves behind a more obstructive collection of tormenting tensions (jealousy, resentment, worry, failure feelings, guilt) than competition which threatens to wound our self-love. Like water used to turn the old mill wheels to grind flour from wheat, so competition is the steady, forceful stream that drives our personalities from birth till death.

Competition, like water, left to the uncontrolled floods of negative thinking can devastate one's self-esteem. But controlled by Possibility Thinking, competition becomes the most dynamic and constructive of the forces that drive our personalities. At birth, the baby cries for food—competing for its mother's attention. The toddler competes with other children for toys. The child competes with one parent for the other parent's attention. Brothers and sisters compete with each other for attention and recognition. In school, the growing child competes against classmates. More than one failure-prone, non-self-loving soul goes tension-torn through life because he willfully chose—in infancy, adolescence, or youth, to deliberately fail and hence avoid competition—which is one of the costs of success.

For sure, this is not the way to handle competition if you ever want deep inner peace. The only way is to recognize that such a reaction will ultimately leave you with the awareness that you copped out on the opportunity to grow to your full potential. And then a deep sense of self-love-shattering shame will haunt you.

The successful secret of handling competition is to use Possibility Thinking! Focus on yourself—not on others. Compete against yourself—and you can't lose! If you lose when you compete against yourself, who wins? You do! Try to better your own previous record of achievement. Keep this up year after year. You'll be astounded at where you will arrive! Not only in personal and professional achievement, but in your mental well-being.

You will have learned to live above the fear of failure! For the person who competes against his own best self, lives beyond the possibility of failure! Remember—*you* always win when you compete against yourself!

2. *Now be your own best booster.* If you knew there was someone conspiring to put you down, you'd know you had an enemy. If this person knocked down your best, brightest, and biggest ideas before they had a fair hearing you'd really be angry.

Right?

Wrong! For there is such a person who treats and has been treating you this way but you quietly, willfully, passively tolerate him! That person who, more than anyone or anything else, puts you down is *you!* For no one else has killed more of your own biggest and best ideas!

"It's impossible," you said silently when that great idea first came into your mind! The truth is you threw out the biggest ideas that ever came into your mind as soon as they arrived. More than anything else this contributes to our less than adequate level of normal achievement. This, as much as any other social, psychological, or spiritual factor contributes to an individual's failure and subsequent lack of self-esteem.

To build a positive self-image start being your own best booster by listening seriously to your own big and bright ideas. Give your dreams a boost with Possibility Thinking and you'll shock yourself and everyone else by watching a fantastic but impossible idea turn a corner and become a possibility. Now let this thinking become a habit, the habit will become a life style, and the life style will crown you with priceless feelings of honorable self-worth.

Waste is always a terrible thing but no waste is more tragic than to waste the best, the biggest, and the brightest ideas God sends your way.

3. *Now discover and develop a philosophy and a plan for dealing with your own imperfections.* When you learn to accept and deal constructively with your imperfections you will make enormous strides in the all-important business of building a mature and secure self-image.

To begin with: strive, but don't pretend to be perfect. Be willing to accept yourself as an imperfect person. Be quick to relax yourself and others by admitting your imperfections. Remind yourself that there is no sinless priest, pastor, or rabbi; there is no perfect, flawless mother; there is no professor who knows all the answers; there is no judge who has never made a mistake. Only Jesus Christ was perfect.

What's very important is that you know—definitely and distinctly—your strengths and your weaknesses. Then determine to reinforce, nurture, and develop to their fullest your personality assets as you forthrightly, frankly, and vigorously face up to your personality liabilities. With a planned persistence try to reduce or eliminate their negative influence in your life. In the

41

process you will not (a) be defensive over your imperfections. Under the fire of criticism from others or from your negative self, you'll respond with a tension-relieving confession: "I know. You're right. This is one of my faults. And I'm working on it. It's challenging and exciting." (b) Be discouraged and defeated if the progress and process toward personal perfection seems slow or even futile. (c) Be hypocritical by pretending that you are someone you aren't. Remember a hypocrite isn't someone who fails to live up to his own standards. That's a definition of a human being. A hypocrite is someone who fails to live up to his own standards, but, with a judgmental attitude, tries to falsely fabricate the impression that he is perfect.

How can you form a responsible appraisal of your strengths and your weaknesses? Find a tried, true, and trusted friend and ask for his evaluation. You'll be amazed at what you hear. For we all tend to distort, in our minds, our self-appraisals. The picture of yourself revealed by an honest critic will be like looking at a photograph someone has taken of you and asking, "Is that what I look like?"

Let me give you a word of warning—and encouragement. You can expect to find that your weakest qualities will lie within your strongest qualities and vice versa. Every person's strength contains weakness. Every person's weakness contains strength.

Humble? Shy!

Quiet? You don't speak up often and loud enough.

Enthusiastic? You talk too much!

Aggressive? You come on too strong!

Forceful? You intimidate people!

How do you handle that? By learning to accept yourself as a growing, emerging, struggling, succeeding, but imperfect human being. And you'll soon become enthusiastic about yourself as an imperfect but really beautiful person.

4. *Forgive yourself for past mistakes.* Learn to forgive yourself for mistakes you made in the past, even if the past is as recent as yesterday. Every day is a new beginning. Remember that God has forgiven you. Now, forgive yourself. Affirm over and over again—God lives within me—God has forgiven me—I have forgiven myself. And when you are tempted to nurse regrets with the destructive phrase, "I wish I had," you will look to the future and say, "Next time I will."

5. *Now accept that part of you that cannot be changed.* Learn to accept yourself. Don't resent the shape of your face or the color of your skin. Don't dislike the sound of your voice or the fact that you are too tall or too short. As a TV pastor, I have interviewed more than one Miss America, and each beautiful girl was well aware of an aspect of her features she thought was a flaw. These physical characteristics are part of you. You can't change them. God created you the way you are because that is the way He intended you to be. Just as no two snowflakes are exactly alike, no two people are identical. You are distinctive. There is only one you and God loves you for what you are. You should too.

6. *Keep on changing yourself for the better.* Try to improve yourself. Your complex personality is many-faceted and bound to change by conditions. You can change for the better or for the worse. And, you have the freedom to choose.

There are people who can't believe that people change: They may believe one can change in the minor areas of life, but not in the major aspects of their character. The truth is *people do change,* and with God's help you can too.

The famous warden of San Quentin prison, Clinton T. Duffy, was responsible for the rehabilitation of many of the men in his charge. He saw a number of them change from hardened criminals who took away from society, into contributing members of the community who gave back more than they had ever taken.

One of the members of the California Adult Authority, the agency in over-all charge of the prison system, was a cynic who really did not believe that you can ever change a person's basic character once it has been firmly set. He verbalized this cynicism with the negative cliché, "Leopards don't change their spots." Duffy's response which silenced his critic was, "I'll have you know that we don't have leopards at San Quentin, we have men. And men can and do change."

Now all persons are less than perfect. You and I have areas where we can improve too. You can resolve to do better in the future, and I predict you will, for you are making an effort by reading a self-improvement book.

Let new circumstances, new commitments and new experiences shape you into the better and more beautiful person you were meant to be!

7. *Now commit yourself to a great cause.* Connect and commit yourself to a cause that, in time, in scope, and in value, transcends your own solitary life. A sense of strong self-identity comes with the feeling of belonging. It may be a political, religious, environmental, or humanitarian cause. Whatever it is, involve yourself in something that is of great importance in the larger scheme of things. Participate. Get out into the limelight. Assume responsibility. You'll generate self-love because responsibility fulfills the need to be needed, and self-love, that wonderful sense of well-being, comes when we know that our life is making a contribution to the human family. There is absolutely no excuse for not

feeling needed in a world where so many hurting and lonely people are desperately hungering for a friendly life, a helping hand, and a listening ear.

8.-*Believe you can succeed.* Nothing builds self-esteem faster than success—nothing deflates self-esteem faster than failure. I have written much on the subject of success because I know how devastating a sense of failure is to a person's self-image. You can be a success if you infuse yourself with a strong belief in your ability to succeed in your private or professional life. Believe you can succeed as a husband or wife, a mother or a father, a member of a community or church group, a political party or participant in sports

You've often heard people say, "I've got to see it before I believe it." That sentence is psychologically untrue. Here's the right way to say it: "I've got to believe it before I can see it." Begin now by building a dream of success for yourself. Remember the words of Thoreau:

If one advances confidently in the direction of his dreams, and endeavors to live a life which he has imagined, he will meet with a success unexpected in common hours.

9. *Dare to love yourself.* Dare to love yourself. Some people are inclined to have a deep suspicion, distrust, and fear of self-love. "I might lose my humility," they think, continuing, "I don't want to become egotistic, snobbish, or arrogant." Three insights must be gained at this juncture:

(a) It is easy for God to humble us, but it is very difficult for Him to keep us believing in ourselves.

(b) The truly self-loving person is inwardly secure and so self-assured that he is naturally, truly, and sincerely humble. Which explains why truly great people are very relaxed and relaxing persons. They put on no airs. They don't need to impress people with their importance. What after all is humility? It is not thinking less of oneself—it is thinking more of others.

(c) The self-loving person dares to be, and so naturally becomes, a very open and transparent person. He is liberated enough to be honestly enthusiastic about himself too.

We may, therefore, misjudge this natural freedom to verbalize positively about himself as a lack of humility on his part. The truth is that *we* then have a problem. He doesn't! We are being judgmental and our false appraisal is in fact a Freudian slip, exposing our own lack of that mature freedom which would allow us to be equally open and honest persons.

10. *Constantly strive to excel in all you do.* Excellence works wonders in strengthening the ego. Every person constantly needs ego nourishment. However, the urge to excellence is not to be mistakenly faulted as an ego trip. It is rather divine worship.

Great opportunities and bright ideas are given by God to us, making us the stewards of these heaven-sent jewels. And our responsibility is to respectfully and reverently receive and polish these divine dreams, turning them into inspiring realities. Then, reporting back to *the source of all creative concepts,* we present to God an accomplishment worthy of a gift to a flawless Lord.

If we are inspired by His Spirit, we will constantly and compulsively be driven to excel. Our basic sincerity will allow us to settle for nothing less than an all-out effort to present to God a polished achievement—without spot, stain, scratch, or wrinkle. The urge to excel is our best effort to develop the God-given gift of a beautiful idea to its fullest and most fruitful potential.

So the pursuit of excellence is our noble art of worship! You glorify God when you build up His sons and daughters. You build yourself up when you return an idea to God and know, deep down in your heart, that though your achievement is not perfect, it does *excel* in competition with yourself!

By contrast, if excellence builds self-worth, mediocrity will shrivel your self-esteem.

Now set high moral standards for yourself, and strive to live up to them. You will gladly and cheerfully accept a temporary "temptation-tension" in exchange for the lasting "peace-of-mind" value which is the ultimate reward of the self-disciplined person who successfully develops great pride-producing moral character through his self-denial and dedication to some beautiful, creative, constructive, inspiring moral ideal!

In the process of building your self-love you'll lift the collective level of self-respect in your community. Even as spectator sports and grand theater succeed because lesser achievers fantasize, identify with, relate to, and imagine themselves as the actor or the athlete, so you—in your moral achievements—will inspire your fellows with pride as they observe your higher, nobler, and uplifting moral dedication.

More than you know you will raise the collective level of society's self-esteem. When the truth hits you that you, one solitary, beautiful person—are to some degree lifting the level of humanity's self-worth then your self-love will be even further enhanced, which is to say that all persons are related to each other.

Yes, all of us are blood relatives. We all are the descendants of the same ancestors—Adam and Eve. Because we are blood relatives that which one person chooses to do will affect the rest of the family in some way or at some time. For instance, if my brother builds

47

an honorable name and reputation I am proud to say, "That's my brother." If he makes a shameful public disgrace of himself, I'm embarrassed.

Therefore, if I commit an act or a deed that—however personally pleasurable or satisfying it may be—is demeaning to myself or to another human, I insult the fellow members of my family. I contribute to the lowering of the collective level of human self-esteem.

The modern philosophy—Let each person do his own thing; it's all right as long as it feels good and doesn't hurt anyone—is illogical, impossible, immeasurably dangerous, and potentially demonic. This reckless pragmatism is only the shallow surmising of a spoiled, selfish, and basically immoral person who rationalizes to get what he wants when he wants it.

Immorality asks the question: "What do I want and enjoy?"

Morality asks the question: "What's right or best?" Each person's morality or immorality will affect the mental well-being of his fellow human beings. We are an organismic unity.

That's why I felt depressed, cheapened, and frightened when I walked past an open door of a Washington hotel room and saw an incredible scene of destruction left by a departing guest. Shattered glass splinters littered the floor, tops of tables as well as chairs, the bed, and davenport! It looked as if dozens of fine wine glasses had been smashed, then scattered like seed.

"Who? Why?" I asked the shocked bellboy who stood inside the room.

"I don't know. I don't understand it," he said sadly.

"What hurts me," I added, "is that this terrible thing was done not by dogs, or horses, or monkeys, but by humans. Fellow human beings. My relatives! They

48

have disgraced me in the process." "Which explains why it's wrong to commit suicide," I explained to my friend Abby Van Buren of "Dear Abby" fame. "Any private act which, becoming public knowledge, comes across like bad news and offends the self-respect of another relative in the human family, is *wrong!* No matter how it may satisfy my personal lust, please my private taste, relieve my individual frustrations, or remove my solitary pain!"

Live a high moral life and you will not only build your own self-love, but in the process you will also build and boost the collective consciousness of self-love in society, and more than you will ever know you will help create a mental climate of collective pride in your community! That's the beginning of the solution to all social problems—crime, injustice, racism, and exploitation! For proud people are slow to stoop to sin.

Prayerfully, carefully, like an archeologist exploring rich ruins to uncover, discover, and recover the priceless and beautiful treasures of a glorious bygone civilization, I challenge you to carefully and prayerfully seek out, in the corridors of grand moral traditions, the highest and noblest moral values. Take them to your heart. Let them become the constitution governing the law of your life. Just as a nation avoids anarchy, waste, and disorder by choosing to be governed not by the whims, wills, and fancies of a time or a thought, but by constitutional law, so your life will not be made a shambles by allowing passing pleasures to plunder your pride. Rather you'll develop a great character which will be crowned and controlled by a conscience that is constrained by God!

11. *Finally, help others build self-love within themselves.* Remember—especially when you are given

rough or rude treatment—every person you meet is having a battle loving himself too.

To really achieve a deep and abiding self-love, start thinking about people around you who need strong supports built under their faltering or battered self-esteem. You'll find that there are many people who are depressed and discouraged. They have not yet learned, as you have, how to build a strong self-love. They have not learned the basic lessons of how to handle competition—how to deal with their dreams—how to cope with their imperfections.

You can help them find the way. Share your success with them. And what a surprising reward will be yours! You'll receive an even more intense awareness that you really are a beautiful person—for sure. You will have practiced and proved the principle: If any person would save his life, he must lose it. And if any person will lose his life, he will find it.

Having achieved a strong self-love, you'll find yourself released from an incredible collection of negative tensions. With a positive self-image, you'll be well on the way to replacing inner stress and strain with inner peace, harmony, power, and creativity.

You'll be well on the way toward being a relaxed and a relaxing person.

III

Relax Tensions Creatively—
Here's How

Of all God's creatures and creations, it is the human being alone who has the inner spirituality capable of being tortured by stress.

Tension is God's way of telling us that we human beings are living, thinking, feeling organisms because we are spiritual creatures.

The minerals that lie under the ground or on the earth's surface feel nothing. Plants react to sun, water, dirt, and fertilizer but despite some limited research findings I don't believe plants respond emotionally to tension. Members of the animal kingdom other than man are insensitive to the complex tensions and emotions that members of the human race experience.

Only human beings are capable of experiencing emotional tension because we are unique spiritual creatures existing in a physical form called a body. If this is a negative—then the positive truth is that we, as "souls in bodies" have the incredible capacity to experience a total dynamic, spiritual relationship. When we achieve harmony between our souls and God, our hearts and minds, we release stress and begin to enjoy life in this fantastic world.

Tensions are symptomatic of disharmony in our spirit. When you have a physical ailment, a doctor will use physical means to cure you. If you have a spiritual sickness such as tension, the cure should be spiritual in nature.

Note well the spiritual attitudes outlined in this chapter, which will put you on the road to easing tension in your life. Follow this program faithfully and you will begin to develop a calm control center at the core of your consciousness.

The first two of the four should be done just before retiring.

1. Ventilate

In this exercise you are going to ventilate your mind. That means you are going to empty your mind of negative, destructive, depressing thoughts and emotions and replace them with clean, fresh, positive, and constructive ideas. Just as by opening a window you flush out the stale, smoky, heavy air from a room and replace it with clear, fresh atmosphere, you'll be doing this with your mind.

Dr. Norman Vincent Peale tells how, early in his career, feeling discouraged one Sunday evening after a poor day during which he thought his sermons were weak, he visited a friend who owned a drugstore. He confided to his friend that he thought perhaps he wasn't cut out for the ministry.

Taking Dr. Peale to the back room where he would mix his mysterious pharmaceutical concoctions the druggist said, "Your problem is that you have allowed your sense of inadequacy, your discouragement, and your feelings of ineffectiveness to accumulate like a pile of garbage in your mind. I suggest that you do what I do at the end of each day. I take all of the accumulated negative emotions that I'm experiencing and opening the windows of my mind I literally ventilate these bad feelings out of my being."

It was wonderful advice. The Bible advises: "Let not the sun go down on your wrath." The meaning of which is—Don't let the hurts and resentments and indecisions of the day go to sleep with you. Otherwise they will awaken with you in the morning, refreshed and stronger than ever in their destructive mastery of your life.

When you go to sleep at night don't carry your failures, worries, guilts, fears, or a sense of inadequacy and discouragement along with you.

Tomorrow's mood is born tonight. Isn't it strange how we humans tend to hang onto the unfortunate experiences, the negative aspects of our lives instead of letting them expire. Indeed, if anything, we nurture them.

On a trip to England, I remember watching huge barges loaded with refuse from the cities being pushed far out to sea by tugs. When they are far enough away from land, levers are pulled and the bottoms of the barges open up to drop the garbage into the depths of the ocean.

In a sense this is what we have to do every night— open up our minds and let the garbage flow out.

How do we do this? By prayer. It is a custom that seems to have been forgotten by many people. There was a time when almost everyone said his or her prayers before retiring. Children were taught simple prayers to repeat before bedtime. When they became adults they carried this tradition with them. Oftentimes families would say their prayers together.

Find a prayer that is meaningful to you. There are many collections of prayers available. Read one of the Psalms. It will give you a prayerful experience.

Get in the habit of ventilating your mind every night. As you do this night after night you'll discover a new feeling of peace coming over you. You'll be emptying out the accumulated misfortunes of the day. Don't try to hang onto them.

Visualize Christ opening the windows of your mind; close your eyes and think of an open window overlooking a beautiful calm sea. The foul air inside rushes out and the fresh, clean sea breeze wafts in. It is crisp, moist, and clear. Now, say your prayers.

2. Anticipate

Now you are ready for exercise number two.

Fill your mind with positive anticipation. Think of the great things you want to accomplish. Tell yourself— tomorrow will be better; it will be a beautiful day. You may want to repeat several times this Bible verse— "Tomorrow the Lord will work wonders among you." (Joshua 3:5)

There was a radio announcer who used to sign off with these words, "No matter who you are, or what your situation is—tomorrow the sun will rise again."

When you awake in the morning focus your thoughts on the positive aspects of your life—your plans, your expectations—the good in your life, not the bad.

Henry Thoreau, the famous author of *Walden*, wrote that every morning he followed the practice of lying awake in bed before he arose and told himself all the good things in life that he could think of. Thoreau would say to himself, "Well, I have wonderful news today—wonderful news. I am alive. That's good news. And I have friends."

The Psalmist said, "In the morning, while the sun rises, I will make my praises unto God."

Every Sunday I open my church service with other words from the Psalms—"This is the day the Lord has made, let us rejoice and be glad in it." I know of no more inspiring statement with which to start the day. I have a friend who unfailingly repeats these words as soon as his feet hit the floor in the morning.

Saturate your mind with all the happy thoughts you can, and you will find yourself enthused with great imagined possibilities.

Exercise your anticipation of great things ahead by repeating positive prayers that are packed with dynamism. Here are two prayers I like to say in this religious exercise:

> Good morning God, I love you.
> What are you up to today?
> I want to be a part of it.
> Thank you, God. Amen.

and

> Lord, show me the person
> you want me to speak to
> through my life today. Amen.

These prayers will also be useful to you as you undertake the third exercise. Positive prayers of this sort put you on the offensive. You will become involved in productive, exciting, and pleasurable projects. When you seek God's guidance in constructive and satisfying work you are surrounding yourself with an invisible shield of tension-deflecting enthusiasm. You will be so engrossed in excellent plans and great ideas that you will be oblivious to the petty annoyances and minor situations that usually produce upsetting tension in an idle mind.

3. Insulate

The society in which we live seems to be steeped in negativism. So many of the people we come in contact with emanate destructive negative vibrations. It becomes vital to insulate yourself from the poisoned darts of negative tension that are aimed at you all through the day.

You know the sinking feeling of disappointment you get when you've suggested something to an associate or friend and you get an immediate negative response. It could be as casual as the suggestion that you see a new movie and the other person answers, "I heard it wasn't very good."

It could be as important as the plan for a new way of doing business and hearing an associate reply, "It won't work—I know someone who tried it and didn't succeed."

If all your thoughts, suggestions, and ideas constantly meet with the sideward shaking of a head and spoken reasons why they aren't any good, you, too, may be drawn into this maelstrom of negativism. It becomes vital that you protect your spirit with an invisible shield that will maintain your positive enthusiasm.

You must learn to protect yourself against doubt, hesitation, and the presentation of reasons why this or that won't work. There are ways this can be done.

To insulate your soul against the tension produced by discouragement, affirm over and over again:

I can do all things through Christ who strengthens me.

To insulate yourself against despair, affirm:

I am persuaded that nothing can separate me from the love of God.

If you are fearful and apprehensive, insulate yourself against worry and concern by affirming:

> The Lord is my light and salvation.
> Whom shall I fear?
> The Lord is the strength of my life.

During World War II an unknown and unnamed Jew forced to flee from his home was hiding in a basement, trying to escape from his Nazi pursuers. He scratched on the wall of his hideout the sign of the Star of David and these three lines:

> I believe in the sun even when it is not shining.
> I believe in love even when I do not feel it.
> I believe in God even when He is silent.

Dr. Daniel A. Poling, the late great Protestant minister who preceded Dr. Peale at Marble Collegiate Church in New York would insulate himself against doubt simply by repeating three times:

> I believe! I believe! I believe!

Why not do the same—so that you will be surrounded by the invisible insulating shield against stress that is the product of a strong and abiding faith.

4. Sublimate

Even though you are faithful in your use of the first three exercises, tension is a very tough foe and you should proceed to this next tension-relieving exercise.

You are going to sublimate the darts of tension that may continue to slip through the shield you are building. In sublimating, your aim will be to turn some of your tensions into positive forces. You must become imbued with the belief that God will let nothing happen to you that you will not be able to turn into a sublime experience. A strong thoroughly convinced possibility thinker is a master of sublimation.

In the middle of the nineteenth century the owner of a beautiful hunting lodge in the north of Scotland invited a group of friends for a weekend of shooting. Just as the weekend opened one of the guests, opening a bottle of soda, splashed some of its contents on a newly painted wall all the way up to the ceiling. The host was quite disturbed and he let the unruly guest know it in no uncertain terms.

The soda made an unsightly mess with an ugly brown spot. All through the weekend the other guests watched as it dried. But before they left, there was little doubt that the wall would have a disfiguring blotch.

All the guests departed with the exception of one. The man who remained behind studied the unattractive wall. Then, using first crayons, then charcoal and finally oil paint, he turned the brown stains into brown highland rocks. Then he painted a stream that splashed its waters over the rocks. At the darkest part of the stain, he put a leaping stag and in the background painted pursuing hunters.

Who was this man who had turned a dirty stain into a beautiful painting? It was Sir Edwin Henry Landseer, the famous English animal artist, best known for the carved stone lions at the base of the Nelson monument, in Trafalgar Square in London.

Eventually the lodge was turned into an inn. Through the years, other artists who have stayed there have added paintings of their own to the walls. Today it is a place of abiding beauty, not a lodge which was almost spoiled by a careless guest.

Turning something ugly or unpleasant into something that is beautiful. That's one kind of sublimation.

Think about the ways you can turn your ugly negative thoughts into beautiful, positive, constructive ideas about life.

That's sublimation and that's using Possibility Thinking to produce peace of mind.

Four Major Tensions That Respond to Sublimation

If you have been trying to lose your tensions and are finding it a very difficult task, think about the possibility of turning your tensions into tools. In other words, if you can't lose your tensions, use them.

When you look up at the sky you'll sometimes see a bird, its wings extended, seemingly floating in space. It isn't moving, and appears to be suspended in the air. What it is doing is leaning against the wind, using the tension or movements of the air to support itself. As the wind blows toward the bird it leans on it. He's resting on it instead of wrestling against it.

When you are at the seashore, watch as the rough waves roll in and break against the jetties, creating noisy, bouncing, rough surf. In the shallow places you'll see people standing, tense and apprehensive, bracing themselves for the fierce slap of the next wave which

59

will come crashing over them. Often they are sent stumbling and sputtering against the gritty, shell-laden bottom.

Off in the distance you'll see others, young golden-skinned boys and girls astride surfboards, rising and falling gently with the undulating waves. They turn their board toward the rising, oncoming waves, stand up, and as a mountainous wave swells to a whitecapped crest, they ride serenely and confidently shoreward, pushed by the power of the same wave that will send other people sprawling onto the sandy beach. The surfers have learned not to fight the waves but to ride them.

Stop deriding and start riding them. Just as the powerful wave can either send you sprawling or carry you forward in smooth, beautiful flight, so, in some cases, can tensions send you crashing down or motivate you to better thoughts and actions. They can make you or break you. Under the grip of their power, you will *grow up* or *blow up*. They can be heavy weights, or gossamer wings. They can shake you—or they can take you—out of a rut. Stop deriding and start riding them.

The 1970 U. S. Open Golf Championship was played at the Hazeltine National Golf Club in Chask, Minnesota. That day was one of the most miserable in the history of the U. S. Open. High winds and an almost freezing temperature made playing extremely difficult. Of all the leading players and champions in the game only one of the eighty broke the course par seventy-two. It was twenty-five-year-old Tony Jacklin, then the reigning British Open champion.

The winds, which were as high as forty-one miles an hour, brought down such champions as Jack Nicklaus, Gary Player, and Bill Casper. Once these giants of golfdom had positioned themselves on the green to putt, the wind would blow them off balance. Arnold Palmer remarked that the reason most of them didn't make par was that they were too cautious because of the wind.

All of the players were; with the exception of Tony Jacklin who, under the circumstances, shot a remarkable seventy-one. What did he do that the others didn't? While the other seventy-nine players tensed up, Jacklin relaxed. While the others were fighting the wind, he was enjoying it and working with it.

"I like playing in this kind of weather," the English player said. "I try to use the wind, not fight it. I let the wind carry the ball to the hole."

That's what you have to do with certain kinds of tensions—don't fight them, use them. Turn them into positive and creative energy.

There are four kinds of tension that respond to this treatment—curiosity tension, adventure tension, temper tension, and boredom tension.

CURIOSITY TENSION

This form of tension produces a state of mental unrest that can be highly destructive. You remember the old adage, "Curiosity killed the cat." Curiosity can also kill humans or destroy them in other ways. It has led many alcoholics to their first drink. Many regular drug users explain the way their habit developed, saying, "I just wanted to try it once to see what it was like."

I remember a newspaper account of an interview with some men on skid row. One of them said, "I came to see the sights. Now I'm one of them."

In the emergency room of a hospital, I saw a young man who had been carried from his wrecked car. "How did it happen?" I asked. "I was curious," he replied. "I just wanted to see how fast it would corner."

"Curiosity has always gotten him into trouble," his worried mother said.

"Not curiosity," I corrected, "but the channels into which the curiosity has flowed."

Curiosity *can* be destructive. *It can also be constructive* if used in the proper fashion.

George Washington Carver became curious about the peanut, following the destruction of the cotton crops by the boll weevil in 1914. Sustained by his faith in God, he discovered that the peanut could produce many by-products to replace those formerly taken from cotton. His work was of tremendous benefit to the American people and to American industry.

Men like Benjamin Franklin, Thomas Edison, and Lee De Forest, were curious about many things. Their discoveries and inventions have made life better and easier for all mankind.

A friend of mine, inventor and researcher Dr. Arnold Beckman said, "God is the sum total of the unknown." There is profound theological truth in that statement. How do you explain man's natural inclination to curiosity? That insatiable, universal human tension we call curiosity is God-implanted in human beings to keep motivating us upward, onward, and outward bound always in search for something more for we intuitively feel that there remains so much yet undiscovered and unexplored in this universe.

This "call of the unknown" is nature's way, yes, God's way of keeping us unsettled, unrested, and uneasy until we make life's greatest scientific discovery—the reality of God who has been to us the Great Unknown.

Curiosity has been the motivating force behind most great explorations and inventions. Curiosity discovered America. Curiosity put men on the moon. Curiosity, along with necessity, might be called the mother of invention. Teachers know that their best students are driven by a deep desire to know more about the areas of knowledge that are hidden from us while we are still young.

So, you see, this tension of curiosity will be terrible or it will be terrific. It depends on the spiritual force that controls you. When the spirit of Jesus Christ controls you, tensions will leave or they will be turned into dynamic, creative energy that can lead you to greater things.

ADVENTURE TENSION

Similar in many ways to curiosity tension is what I call adventure tension. Those who have adventure tension may well be driven into committing all kinds of evil acts—crimes, sexual exploits, and perversions. Wars have been launched by unstable rulers who sought release and fulfillment by entering into such adventurous situations.

Teen-agers take joy rides for adventure, only to be picked up for auto theft. Men and women enter into illicit relationships with the husbands and wives of others in a quest for the excitement of adventure.

However, when God's great spirit takes over, the tension of adventure becomes a great motivating force. A scientist is motivated to spend long hours with his microscope, peering into the miniworld of the microbe and virus. He unceasingly experiments with new approaches, new formulas, new chemicals in a relentless search for cures, vaccines, and answers to the challenge of disease.

Adventure curiosity opens new worlds to the young. I remember when I took my oldest child to the airport to start her on her way to her first year at college. She had kissed her mother, brother, and sisters good-by. We were alone together in the auto on the way to her plane. Both of us were quiet until she spoke.

"You know what I've been thinking, Dad?" she said.

I shook my head, and she said, "I've been thinking about some lines you once quoted." And then she repeated them. "Grieve not for me who am about to start a new adventure. Eager I stand and ready to depart, me and my reckless pioneering heart."

Two good friends of mine were the late Dorothy and Henry Poppen, who spent over forty years in China, building schools, hospitals, and churches. There was always great risk involved. Disease was endemic, the roads were treacherous, bandits roamed the countryside. Finally they were captured by the Communists and imprisoned. They eventually escaped and made their way to the United States. They had to leave behind their schools and hospitals.

"What drove you all those years?" I asked Mrs. Poppen.

"We thrived on adventure," she replied, her eyes afire with the thought of their years of excitement.

A person driven by adventure tension can become very dangerous unless he has the moral restraint and guiding rule of God's spirit. Without the hand of God he can become a criminal or a rogue, a force for evil in the world.

Those who are driven by adventure tension and who are inspired by the spirit of Jesus Christ can become among the most dynamic persons in the world.

Would we be better off if the feelings of anger that so often assail us could be permanently removed? It would be foolish to think so. Temper often turns soft iron into hard steel. Take the temper away and often the will is weakened.

Like curiosity and adventure tension, temper tension can drive a person to destroy himself and those around him or it can lead to greatness. Once again, it depends upon the spirit that moves the temper-tense person.

In the officers club at the Grant Heights Air Force Base in Japan I noticed a young officer at the next table doing card tricks. I soon learned that he was a professional magician.

"How did you become a magician?" I asked.

He laughed as he answered, "When I first joined the Air Force, I got into a card game and lost my entire paycheck. Later I found out that the winner was a card shark. I was mad. I vowed I'd get even. I decided to learn every card trick there was and use them. While this was happening I also learned how stupid it was to gamble and I also discovered that I am not the kind of person who could really cheat in an honest game. By that time, having learned all the card tricks, I found I was in demand as an entertainer. Last year I earned more than three thousand dollars, performing at parties in the Tokyo area."

Somehow you, too, can turn your temper tensions into springboards for productive opportunities.

BOREDOM TENSION

H. L. Mencken, the great newspaper editor and author, once wrote, "The capacity of human beings to bore one another seems to be vastly greater than that of any other animals."

Psychiatrists, in the jargon of the profession, say that boredom comes when one is dissatisfied with stimuli proffered and desires other stimuli.

The Duke de la Rochefoucauld, the famous epigrammatist, stated, "We forgive quite readily those who bore us but we never forgive those who are bored by us."

Field Marshall Ligne said, "I don't get bored by myself; it is others who bore me."

Samuel Butler, the author of *The Way of All Flesh,* suggested that a person who lets himself be bored is even more contemptible than a bore.

Boredom apparently is, and has been, a subject of much discussion and investigation. More than that, boredom is one of the more destructive influences in people's lives. The tension that comes from boredom is responsible for many of the problems that confront us today.

Boredom is a prime cause of alcoholism, drug addiction, pornography, gambling, and sexual promiscuity. In our affluent society, with its overwhelming amount of leisure time, boredom can create havoc in the life of many persons.

However, when the spirit of Jesus Christ comes into a bored life, many amazing things happen. With Jesus to guide you:

Boredom becomes a tension waiting to be channeled into creative areas.

Boredom is a clean blackboard offering its surface to be written on.

Boredom is a silent organ awaiting a skillful hand on its keys to produce great sounds.

Boredom is a loving heart longing for its chance to share hopes and dreams.

Boredom is a brilliant mind, standing empty, waiting to be filled with tremendous ideas.

How can boredom tension be turned into inspiring activity?

Possibility Thinking will do it. The belief that you can do something bigger and better with your life than drinking, playing, gambling, overeating, or wasting your hours on idle thoughts and dull chatter.

When Jesus Christ inspires you with a beautiful dream of what can be and mountain moving faith triggers you into action, boredom is changed into dynamic commitment.

Try and keep trying to probe for positive possibilities in the negative experiences of life and your tensions will turn into springboards, lifting you to action for good.

Now try to use the Possibility Thinking Power of sublimation to handle the collection of tensions that can best be described as "hurts that roost in your memory nest."

See the next chapter to see how you can turn your scars into stars!

IV

Turn Your Scars into Stars

Is it possible to draw a pension from our tension? To turn this enemy into a friend? To turn our scars into stars? Can we sublimate the collection of hurts in our memories that rob us of peace of mind?

"Out of your weakness shall come strength," a wise man once wrote. (Hebrews 11:34)

That is like saying where a bone is broken, it knits, welds together, and heals, and it becomes stronger at that point.

It is like saying that where flesh is cut and the tissues heal, the skin mends, and a scar is formed. It then becomes tougher than any other point on the surface of the body.

A guide said to me some years ago in the Netherlands as we walked across a dike, "See that huge concrete plug? That is where we had a leak at one time and the sea rushed in. Many people perished, but we plugged it with steel-reinforced concrete. It will never break there again."

Where you are weak, there you will be made strong.

A doctor said to me one time as he pointed to a nurse walking down the hallway, "She is the best nurse we have. How she works! She is so dedicated." Then, as an afterthought he said, "It is because when she was a

69

teen-ager she spent ten months on her back in this hospital."

Out of your weakness can come strength.

There is a key principle here: If you want to live an emotionally healthy and happy life you have to know how to handle the hurts that come.

There are, if I may suggest, six or seven forms of hurts that make strike us:

There is such a thing, for instance, as being hurt by your friends.

And we all know what it is like, I suppose, to be hurt by an enemy.

There is a third type of hurt and that is the self-inflicted wound for which you later hate yourself.

Hurts from friends,

Hurts from enemies,

Hurts that are self-inflicted.

There are others that you can only say life threw at you.

A bridge collapses and you get hurt. You can't pin the blame on anyone. At a time like that there is always the temptation to blame God. Be careful. The odds are that a human being made a mistake and that is why it happened.

There are those hurts that are caused by God. A husband is taken home. God took him and you are hurt. Yet when you married him, God never promised you how long you could have him, it was simply for better or for worse—"till death do us part." It might have been for a day, it might have been for a week, maybe a month, perhaps a year, ten years or more. God made no promises.

The book of Hebrews advises to turn your weakness into strength.

How do you do that?

I suggest it could be done with four principles—four things to keep in mind in order to handle life's hurts:

1. Don't curse them;
2. Don't rehearse and nurse them;
3. Disperse them (I will show you how);
Finally,
4. Reverse them! Turn them inside out until the hurt becomes a halo, and the scar becomes a star!

DON'T CURSE THEM!

I hear it all the time: "See her," they say, "she has been drinking a lot ever since she lost her husband." Or they point to him and they say, "You know, he has been going downhill ever since his boy died." Or they say, "Oh, he dropped out of high school when he was a senior because he didn't make the football team. That did it." Or they point and say, "I think I'm going to have to let her go, she is just not doing her work. Ever since she didn't get the promotion, she hasn't been much good to the company."

There are many ways of cursing our hurts. Curse them and you become bitter. Anytime somebody is hurt he either becomes a bitter person or a better person. Don't curse them.

DON'T REHEARSE THEM AND NURSE THEM!

A lady who is a dear friend called on me recently. Her husband had passed away two years ago. The poor, dear soul—how I wished she had come in sooner. She waited so long—two long, suffering, painful years, alone, crying inside, killing herself with grief.

She had been rehearsing the way it happened! How he had acted eight weeks before he had his heart attack;

71

six weeks before, four weeks, and three. Then she recalled what he had done the week before the attack and, finally, the fatal morning. She had been rethinking the scene over and over again. Then she said, as she opened her large purse and took out her billfold, "I have something here that I always carry with me. I wanted to know just why he died. So I asked the doctor, couldn't they have tried electric shock to start his heart, or something?" The doctor gave her a very technical, clinical definition of how he had died. She said, "I copied it on this piece of paper and I carry it with me all the time."

She showed it to me. I don't remember the words exactly, but it was something to this effect: "Your husband's condition started because of an inner problem in the arteries which became clogged, then blood clots formed, and finally one of the large clots got so large that it closed off the whole passage so that the blood could no longer flow into the heart. When that happened the valve closed off and then an enormous pain came. Then the lungs no longer were able to expand and then he died from a failure of oxygen." Et cetera.

I almost cried because I love her very much. Well, I said a prayer with her and God performed a healing in my study.

I then said to her, "Now, I want to say one final thing before you leave. One last piece of advice." She said, "Certainly, Pastor, anything you say." I said, "I want you to take that piece of paper and tear it up and throw it away. Don't ever look at it again." She said, "Do you really think that is what I should do?" I said, "I know that is what you should do." She said, "Okay, Pastor, I'll do that." And I am sure she did.

If you nurse and rehearse your hurts, you will finally

develop what psychologists call a neurosis, an abnormal attention to a compulsive emotion, and that will make you sick.

DISPERSE YOUR HURTS!

Don't nurse and rehearse them, but disperse them. Here's how:

You probably can't help it when the hurt comes, but you can help it if the hurt lasts. Through the power of God and through the power of prayer you can handle any hurt. I know this is true. But you have to pray the right way.

A friend of mine was having a business problem with a competitor and all kinds of negative emotions were coming in. I suggested that he pray about it. He said, "What do I pray? Do I pray that the guy will succeed?" I said, "Well, I don't know, just pray that God will tell you what to pray. Ask God what to pray for."

This week he told me, "I woke up at two o'clock in the morning and I had the prayer." I said, "What was it?" He said, "This was the prayer: Dear God, make that person into exactly the person you want him to be and cause his business to develop just the way you would like to see it develop. Amen."

My friend continued, "That just completely cured me. Now, if that guy's business succeeds, I can't possibly be angry about it. I know God wants it to go. Of course, if he goes bankrupt—well, I will be able to face that, too." He was very sincere:

"God, make him the person you want him to be and cause his business to develop the way you want it to develop."

If you have a hurt and if you have prayed about it,

and your prayer hasn't helped you, then you have prayed the wrong prayer. Start by asking God what you ought to pray about.

Archbishop Fulton Sheen spoke about hurts from the pulpit of our church not long ago. The archbishop has had some personal deep hurts. He said, "I was able to find peace when I realized that ultimately nothing ever happened unless God at least permitted it." What a profound statement.

To really get rid of your hurts, you have to look deep into your own self.

Somehow you have to find at what point you yourself were at fault.

If you have a problem with a person, I am sure it is not completely the other person's fault.

The hardest and the most healing word in the Bible is the word repent. That may be what you need to do.

You can disperse your hurts if your relationship with God is right.

Are you suffering from a hurt that is self-inflicted?

Do you hate yourself for what you have done?

Maybe you are cheating on your wife, or your wife is cheating on you;

or you are stealing from your employer;

or you are dishonest and you hate like Hades the man you see in the mirror.

"Oh, God," you say to yourself, "if there were just some way to tear the black page out and start over again!"

There is! That is possible! You can disperse your hurt!

Say, "Jesus Christ, take me, cleanse me, forgive me, and I know, God, if you forgive me I will be able to live with myself."

Start over fresh and clean!

How do you handle your hurts? Don't curse them, don't rehearse and nurse them, disperse them.

REVERSE YOUR HURTS!

Turn your hurts inside out and

> Turn the problem into a project,
> The enemy into a friend,
> The hurt into a halo,
> The scar into a star.

The more I read about, and the more I touch great people, the more I am convinced of one thing. There is no great person alive who has not been hurt deeply.

I am so convinced of this that I recently found myself praying this amazing prayer:

God, hurt me more so that I can help people more.

Years ago I was invited to preach at Marble Collegiate Church. Dr. Peale was, and still is, the senior pastor of that church, but at that time the evening preacher was Dr. Daniel A. Poling. When I arrived I didn't have my pulpit robe with me. Looking for one that would fit me, one of the officials reached into the closet and said, "Here, Dr. Dan's (Poling) should fit you." I slipped into it, and as I did, one of the buttons came off. I put it in my pocket. Later that week back home in California I mailed it with a letter to Dr. Poling. "My apologies, sir," I wrote, "but here is a button off your robe."

I got a letter back that you wouldn't believe. It was fantastic! Remember that I was just an unknown youth, only a few years away from an Iowa farm. Dr. Poling wrote: "The loss of a button is a cheap price to pay for the honor of having you wear my robe, good sir."

Later on I learned the secret of Dr. Poling's greatness. In World War I he was a chaplain. He ran between trenches one hundred yards apart. At one point a hail of bullets surrounded him . . . others fell dead . . . he came out alive. In another instance he was one of four men carrying a litter on which was a German prisoner with mangled legs. A shell exploded in the mud nearby. The others were blown to pieces, but Dr. Poling lived.

Then, of course, you may have heard about Clark, Dr. Poling's son. Clark was a teen-age student in a private high school located out of the city. He sent a telegram saying, "Dad, I am coming home this weekend. I want to see you alone. Meet me at the depot." Dr. Dan met his son at the depot wondering what kind of trouble his boy was in.

Together they went into an office at Marble Collegiate Church. When the boy noticed there was no lock he took a chair and put it under the door knob so that nobody could interrupt their conversation.

"By this time," Dr. Dan said later, "I was really trembling inside. I sat behind my desk and my boy came and pulled a chair right up next to mine and then put his elbows on top of my desk. He put his chin in his hands and just looked. Now," the father continued, "I made many mistakes in my life, but I didn't make a mistake here by asking what was wrong . . . I just waited.

"Finally, my boy looked up at me and said, 'Dad, tell me what do you know about God?'

"I looked at him and said, 'What do I know about God? Very little, my son, very little. But enough to change my whole life!'

"The boy looked at me and said, 'That's good enough, Daddy, that's good enough. I think I'll be a preacher like you when I grow up.' And he did. He graduated from seminary, married, and had a beautiful little baby."

On December 7, 1941, when bombs fell on Pearl Harbor, Clark came to his dad and said, "Dad, I am going to enlist as a chaplain. The only problem is, I think that is taking the easy way out." Dr. Dan looked at his son and said, "Don't you say that, son. I will have you know that in the First World War the most dangerous post that you could have was the post as chaplain. On a percentage basis more chaplains died in the First World War than even the infantrymen . . . one out of ninety-three, to be specific. If you become a chaplain, you may have your chance to die, Clark."

Clark became a chaplain. His father was in London when he heard the news that the S.S. *Dorchester*, a troop ship with over nine hundred on board had been torpedoed off Greenland with only a handful of survivors. The rest had gone down with the ship. On board were four chaplains. Then he read the newspaper report that one of the survivors said that as the ship was about to slip beneath the cold waters, he saw the four chaplains, each was unstrapping his life preserver and handing it to a soldier who then jumped into the sea and was saved. Having given up their life preservers, the four chaplains—two Protestants, a Catholic, and a Jew—kneeled in prayer as the ship slipped beneath the water taking the chaplains with it. One of those four was Clark Poling.

From that time Dr. Dan's heart grew so big that he wanted to take in every boy on planet earth. He wanted to be Dad to everybody.

Turn your scars into stars.

It can make you a better person or a bitter person. It depends on you.

Reverse them. Turn your hurt into a halo.

One day as I stepped out of my office and watched the elevator doors open, I saw a young mother with her little daughter pulling at her skirts. The mother looked busy—she seemed to be rushed, a little harassed. She had her hands so full that she could not help her little girl. I asked my secretary, "Who is she?" My secretary reminded me that she was in charge of our Helping Hand project.

She has spent many hours collecting tin cans of soup and beans. People call into our telephone counseling center, New Hope, twenty-four hours of the day. It is the first twenty-four-hour live telephone counseling program in the United States operated by volunteers and members of the church. When people call and tell us they have nothing we will supply them with groceries, clothing, sometimes even housing.

This young mother of five who is so busy with her family devotes hours every week managing this whole operation. Only a few people know how much work and time is involved. I commented on that and my secretary said, "You remember she wrote you a letter that really moved you a few years ago." It read:

"Dear Dr. Schuller: I can't begin to thank you for your congregation. What wonderful Christians they are. My husband has been flat on his back in bed for months and can't work. I had a baby who became sick and I couldn't work. The church heard about it and the ladies came and brought us breakfast, dinner, and supper. They did this day after day, week after week. How can I ever repay you? How can I ever repay them?"

She has found a way.

Again and again, when I look at a great person I think, sometime that person was hurt.

Or perhaps he was so close to seeing other people hurt that he hurt with them.

You *can* turn your hurt into a halo.

You may know about the royal palace in Teheran, Iran. I was there not long ago. I have been in royal palaces around the world, but this one was something else. There isn't anything like it, to my knowledge, any place in the world.

You step into the royal palace and the grand entrance is just resplendent with glittering sparkling glass. You think for a moment that the domed ceilings and the side walls, and the columns are all covered with diamonds, and not cut crystal; however, they are all small pieces of mirrors. The edges of the myriad of little mirrors reflect light, throwing out the colors of the rainbow. A mosaic of mirrors!

Spectacular!

Here's how it happened: When the royal palace was planned, the architects ordered mirrors to cover the entrance walls from a firm in Paris. When the mirrors arrived it was found that they had all been broken in transit. There were thousands of pieces of smashed mirror. They were going to dispose of them all when one creative man said, "No, maybe it will be more beautiful because they are broken."

More beautiful because they were broken? He took some of the larger pieces and smashed them also and then he fitted them together like an abstract mosaic. If you ever see the palace, you will note that there is an enormous distortion in its reflections, sparkling with rainbow diamond colors.

Broken to be made beautiful!

Do you have a hurt?

If you do, turn it over to God and

He will turn it inside out.

He will reverse it and it will become a star instead of a scar in your crown!

V

After Grief Come Alive Again

The deepest scar, and potentially the most painful of all tensions is grief that follows the resented removal—by death—of a loved one from your life.

Because this peace and joy shattering experience is universal and because if it is handled incorrectly it can produce a morbid and myriad mass of additional destructive emotions, we will deal with grief specifically and at length.

The extreme hunger pangs that signal emotional starvation—that's what grief is. Every person needs physical, emotional, and spiritual nourishment or he will suffer the starvation that inevitably follows deprivation. The good news I have is that starvation, caught in its early stages, is reversible.

What emotional strengths did I draw from the one who is now and forever removed, is a question that must be asked. Friendship? Love? Courage? Perhaps your major supply line of necessary ego fulfillment has been suddenly and brutally severed. It may cause you to plunge into an identity crisis. "Who am I now? She needed me, but now nobody needs me," your confused heart cries out. So new sources of emotional reinforcement must be found. Which explains why a beautiful friendship and personal relationship with God proves to be the answer. From that perspective I have ten words of counsel.

1. *Face grief's fearsome phase.* As a pastor for over a quarter of a century I have witnessed people's reactions to grief and have observed how, in almost every case, there are several related tensions connected with that emotion grief. Often the related tensions unfold as grief passes through several phases.

A. *Unbelief.* "It's not really happening." "He can't be dead. He's coming back tomorrow!" "I can't believe it's really happening." "This can't be true! It must be a nightmare. I'll waken tomorrow and find this was a bad dream."

Unbelief is the first fearsome face and phase of grief. This unbelief is, of course, an effort to reject and deny the reality of what has happened. Counseling must often be directed at causing the mourners to face up to the irreversible reality of the death of their loved one. I often have, therefore, begun my counsel to the survivors with the comment, "I'm so sorry. Now understand this—your loved one is gone. He is dead—to this life. Nothing can change that. But you can control your reaction to what has happened. You will decide what this will do to you. It will either make you into a better person or a bitter person. But you must accept the reality of what has happened."

B. *Regret.* "Why didn't I?" "If only I had." This is grief's second phase. Remorse will pass away in time: Regrets, on the other hand, must be dealt with. Talk them out to a comforting friend.

C. *Guilt.* Now grief moves into the guilty phase. "It's my fault." There is always guilt mixed in with grief. Because this is so prevalent we shall deal with it in depth later in this chapter.

D. *Anger.* Almost always anger follows guilt. "It's

not fair," is the feeling. And now it is natural and normal to be angry at God. All right! Tell Him you're angry. Verbalize it. Then ask for His forgiveness. He understands. He will heal you! It is no sin to be angry with God. It's natural. It is a sin not to share this with Him.

E. *Self-pity* is the next phase of grief. "Why me?" "What did I do to deserve this?" Here it is well to counsel with the honest words: "Who do you think you are to be so spared from grief? It is an inevitable event in all meaningful relationships. But self-pity will destroy something within you. That you must not let happen. A Greek tragedy has the mourner saying over the body of her dead husband: 'The death thy death hath dealt to me is worse than the death that death hath dealt to thee.' This turns a single death into a double tragedy! It's unnecessary. It's irresponsible. It's wasteful. It must not happen."

F. *Depression.* "I don't care any more." This is usually the bottom level of grief. You will not allow yourself to remain in this depression. You will now enter

G. *Grief's final phase—and that's renewal.* Depression is often the darkness before the dawn. "Weeping may endure for a night but joy comes in the morning."

Jeremiah, the "weeping prophet" of the Bible was in a deep depression phase when he said: "My soul is bereft of peace. I have forgotten what happiness is." (Lamentations 3:17) Then suddenly God moved into Jeremiah with thoughts and Jeremiah found renewal! New life! Listen to him now as he starts to climb out of the darkness: "But this I call to mind and therefore I have hope the steadfast love of the Lord never ceases, His mercies never come to an end; They are new every morning; Great is thy faithfulness." (Lamentations 3:21, 22, 23)

When you suffer from the tension of grief remember that you can and must think and act responsibly to control it. Reshape and remold your thinking. There is relief from grief when you put the past behind and look to the promise of the future. But first—make sure you give yourself a good cry!

2. *Open up—or blow up.* The tension of grief, like all tension, must find release or it can and will produce serious and even mysterious and seemingly unrelated. problems.

When unbearable grief descends upon you it is very normal for you to want to have a good cry. This is true for men as well as women, although some men feel that crying is a sign of weakness. Not so. Don't be afraid to cry. If there are no tears in your eyes, you will tear yourself up inside. Your grief will stay bottled up in your inner being. The inclination to weep is nature's built-in release valve to allow you to exhaust your tension.

Express your grief and find emotional relief from grief by letting your tears flow. It is healing weeping. A good healthy cry is not an indication of "little faith" or weakness. God created you with this inclination. Let yourself go and have a good cry. Then you'll find new strength, calmness as you recover with renewed poise.

Now that you've had a good cry give yourself a good try—at coming alive again.

We have all heard stories of young men and women who have lost a beloved just before they were to have been married and spent the rest of their lives in mourning, never to marry. Romantic as this kind of behavior may seem, it is neither healthy nor in keeping with God's wishes. God has promised you: Behold, I make all things new. (Revelation 21:5) God wants you to have a new life. Begin it with bright, new, positive thoughts. Say to yourself—it is possible to enjoy life again.

There is always a way when you really try. The three letters of that powerful word TRY stand for:

T rust— Believe there is a way.

R each—Reach out in different directions. Make new discoveries. Create new interests. Find new friends.

Y ield— Yield to God's will. We do not always understand but be sure that He has a plan for new happiness for you. Yield to God's happy new plan for you.

3. *Let new thoughts make you a new person.* So you try to come alive again by throwing out old grief thoughts that would hold you down and keep you down. It is always painful to dispose of the clothes, and things left behind by a departed loved one. But it must be done. You must go through the closets, empty the drawers, and take charge of affairs. Likewise—go through your mind and clear out old thoughts that have to be dealt with.

After your period of mourning, you must get set to forget. Yes, you must be willing to forget your lost love or your lost parent, child, sibling, or friend. Does that sound cruel? You would probably feel guilty if you really forgot. The truth of the matter is that grief-stricken people do not want to forget. They believe that as long as they remember they will not have completely lost the person whose physical presence has left them.

To a widow I was counseling, I said, "You have never really accepted the passing of your husband. You must do so. Have you ever said to yourself or to others, 'My husband passed away'?"

"No," she replied.

I then told her, "You must. I am going to make you say it. Repeat these words after me. My husband has passed away."

Although it obviously was painful for her to do it, she repeated the words.

Then I said, "Now will you please tell your departed husband something." I suggested that she say out loud the following words:

"Honey, ever since you have been gone, the only person I have been loving is you. I have got to stop loving you because while I have been loving you, especially since you have been gone, I have not been loving other people as I should. Honey, I've got to start forgetting you. I know you understand."

I suggested that she repeat these words over the next few weeks. By articulating, she began to understand that her life had not ended and that God wanted her to live again. It was proving to be effective spiritual therapy. Soon she started to come alive.

In the course of counseling I asked her this question, "Since your husband has been gone, do you feel you love him more than you loved him when he was alive?"

She said, "Yes, I do."

I then asked, "Have you had a fight with him since he died?"

"What do you mean?" she asked.

"Have you had an argument with him in your heart since his funeral?"

"Of course not," was her answer.

"You did have arguments with him when he was alive, didn't you?" Her answer was in the affirmative.

"So the love you have felt for him since his passing is not a realistic love," I pointed out. "It is not a rational love, not even an intelligent love. It is a neurotic love.

Since he has been gone you can't think of anything he ever did that was wrong. It's time to start a new life and discover new love through new thoughts."

If you are grieving now, start to bury thoughts of the past. Worn, depressing, and mournful thoughts must be cast out. *Remember that old thoughts make moldy people.* Remove yourself from the stale, musty, stultifying influence of the sorrows of the past.

Stop nursing, coddling, caressing, and embracing those memories. Like narcotics, visions of the past create false, unrealistic illusions of reality. Under their hypnotic spell you will be living in a dreary dream world of negative fantasy.

Yesterday is past. Today is a new day filled with God's new mercies. Think your way to a bright new life with bright new thoughts.

4. *Replace false thoughts with true thoughts.* Jesus promised, "You shall know the truth and the truth shall make you free."

Two primary false thoughts that enter the mind of grief-stricken thinking:

I'll never get over this. Wrong. You may never be exactly the same person because of what has happened but the hurt will heal eventually. You will get over it.

I've lost everything. Wrong again. You have not *lost* someone, you've been separated from him or her.

Doris Day, known to millions for her many enjoyable movies, went through the agonies of grief when her husband passed away several years ago. At the time she shared her deep feelings with me and told me how she had returned to life.

"My son, Terry, helped. I was sitting in my bedroom in Palm Springs. And I was crying. Terry came in and I said to him, 'I wish I could be strong like you.' He then asked me if I really wanted to be strong. I said I did.

87

Then, he said, 'You can be. Stop crying. Start working. You can keep on crying for ten years but it won't do any good. You can do that or you can stop right now.'

"Then my faith really came alive. I had been reading the words of Christ in my Bible for years. I recalled His promise. 'He who lives and believes in me shall never die.' It hit me with enormous force. God promises eternal life.

"I found I was asking myself, Doris Day, do you believe the Bible and Jesus Christ? If so stop storing those words away and start using them. If you store food in a cupboard, it will rot. Use it and it will nourish you.

"It dawned on me—if I didn't start applying God's promise, I'd be a fool. I don't want to be a fool.

"Today I have no sense of grief. I see my loved ones on the other side. They are smiling, saying to me, 'You're right, you're right.' "

She ended her story by saying, "When you are riding in an airplane and hit an air pocket, the plane drops and you gasp. But the plane rises. It comes back up. So it is when a loved one passes on. You drop. You gasp. But soon you feel the uplifting power of God's renewing spirit."

If your life has been stopped by the tension of grief, take courage from this experience that Doris Day had. It *is* possible to return to a joy-filled, active life and to find, once again, the clouds parting and the sun shining through.

5. *Think about what you have left, not what you have lost.*

Never use that negative word "lost." The very word is an emotional bomb. You cannot verbalize it or hear it without being weakened to some degree by it. The subconscious mind does not have the power to sift out the logical from the illogical. So emotionally charged words only confuse your thinking. Avoid especially all words that are intrinsically and relatively negative. "Lost" is such a word. I recall in my youthful ignorance I wrote to Dr. Daniel A. Poling expressing my condolences upon the death of his wife. I used that ugly word "lost." He replied with the customary courtesy but his answer vastly affected me. "My dear wife is not lost. She is gone and I know where I can find her."

When someone near and dear is gone, one of the remarks heard most frequently is "I've lost *everything*." Yet, there is never any situation in life in which *everything* is lost.

A widower made that remark to me one day shortly after his wife had died. I asked him to sit down and review with me the pluses in his life. Did he have children? Yes, he did but they were grown and married and he didn't see them very often. But he did love them and they did visit him from time to time. Did he have friends? Yes, he did but, of course, they weren't as close to him as his wife had been.

The fact remains that he hadn't lost everything. There were still a great many people in his life. Today he is happily married again!

Why do so many people have a tendency to review what they do not have or what they've lost rather than what they still have? It is a form of negative thinking—a form of impossibility thinking.

Do not dwell on what's gone. Think only of what you have. Your life will be much happier. You'll be dispersing the clouds of the tension of grief.

A woman who had never married and was now old came to me and made a similar remark, "I'm losing everything I have."

"You never lose everything," I replied. "At the least, there is always one person left. I am that person. I will

89

never forsake you. In any event, there is always Jesus Christ. He will never forsake you."

6. *Forgive yourself.* Guilt always seems to be mixed with grief.

When one who is close to you dies, you begin to feel that in some way you may have been responsible. You might say to yourself, "I should have called the doctor sooner," or, "If I only had not left him or her alone," or "Why didn't I realize . . ." or "Why didn't I insist . . ."

Any number of ideas flow through your mind as you relate the death to something you did or didn't do. In practically every situation there is no truth in the thought.

At a funeral service I once conducted for the husband of a very happily married couple, the widow fell over the casket and cried out, "Forgive me, forgive me! Why did I go out partying and leave you alone so often?"

As I led her away, I tried to reason with and placate her, but it was impossible for me to communicate.

In the weeks that followed she became a very sick woman. She stopped living, keeping to herself much of the time, refusing to see any of her old friends.

On a visit I asked, "Have you forgiven yourself yet?"

"What do you mean?" she said.

"Do you remember what you said just before leaving your husband's casket?" I asked. She had no idea what I was referring to.

When I told her what she had said, she was astonished.

"I didn't say that, did I?"

She had apparently buried, deep in her unconscious mind, the words as well as the thoughts that had provoked her remark. When she heard me repeat what she had said, she began to recall the guilt that she had hidden in the deep recesses of her mind. Once she was able to do that she was able to come to grips with the feeling of guilt and dispose of it.

The truth is that none of us really give the time, attention, and affection to our loved ones that we feel we should. As a practical matter, if we did, we would become overindulgent and that in itself would not be a healthy situation. The feeling of guilt is understandable, but it is essential that you forgive yourself.

7. *Toughen your mind.* Grief quickly spawns self-pity as you begin to ask, "Why did this happen to *me?*"

Your heart may be broken but you are going to have to be tough on yourself. You absolutely must cast out the stifling effects of self-pity that cause the tension of grief to linger indefinitely.

Too often self-pity is generated, nourished, and sustained by the sincere sympathy of friends and relatives. They feel they are supporting you by extensive and continuing understanding. But instead of strengthening you their sympathetic words tend to feed your self-pity.

During a call on a woman who had lost her husband many months before, I began my conversation by assuring her that I had only love for her and sincerely wanted to help. But then I told her, "The only way I can help you is to hurt you. Do you want me to help?"

She nodded in assent.

"I must be blunt," I said. "You have had plenty of time to express your sorrow and grief. You are now indulging in self-pity. Self-pity is a negative emotion. It weakens you and saps your being of the strength to live joyously. Get tough with yourself. Stop acting like a baby. Grow up!"

It was rough talk but the verbal slap shocked her into considering what she was doing to herself. It worked. She started to build a new life.

Consider this—nobody else is going to be as rough on you as you must be on yourself. To rid yourself of self-pity you must talk to yourself in no uncertain terms. Be tender when it comes to forgiving yourself but be tough when you are dealing with self-pity.

It isn't easy to overcome self-pity. How do you do it?

Start by asking: "Who do I think I am that I should be spared this tragedy? It happens to many people every day of the year. It happens to the rich, the poor, the privileged and underprivileged. The contented and the discontented.

"Some of the most towering figures in the Bible, those who were closest to God, suffered similar tragedies."

Then, talk tough. Tell yourself: "You're acting like a child. Grow up now. You're an adult and you've got to act like one. Straighten up and get over this tragedy. You have many days ahead of you. Do you want to live them in misery or in joy?"

Give yourself a good dressing down every day until the pangs of self-pity within you are driven out.

8. *Watch out for your worst enemy.* I know a man whose only child was drowned at an early age. From that point on he blocked God from his mind. He became a professed atheist.

When he was in his late fifties a series of events led him to a strong religious faith. After several years of disappointing personal and business experiences, he found himself sunk in a deep depression, wallowing in unceasing misery. In desperation, he dialed the letters NEW HOPE on his telephone. That carried his voice to an attendant at the twenty-four-hour counseling service the Garden Grove Community Church maintains at the top of our fifteen-story Tower of Hope on the church grounds.

Starting with the spiritual counseling he received that night he began to find a faith he had never known before. From that faith in God he perceived things about himself he'd never realized.

His testimony today, "All through the fifty-six years of my life my greatest enemy has not been a person. It has been a word. What is the word? It is why. Why? Why? Why? I have spent time continually asking that question about everything that has happened to me. After years of misery I made the greatest discovery of my life. It is that life is meant to be enjoyed, not figured out."

Why? That's one question God never answers. Even Jesus Christ, dying on the cross, asked it. "God, my God, why have you forsaken me?"

The reason God will never answer that question is that it indicates an unwillingness on our part to accept the tragic realities of life. He knows that we really don't want an explanation, we want an argument.

When a parent tells a child to do something, often the child will respond with, "Why do I have to do it?" But he doesn't want an explanation. He is looking for a way out, a way not to comply. In the same way God will not answer the question of "why." He will not be drawn into an argument. He does not have to give us His reasons. We must throw out the "why" when we are faced with tragedy.

Your worst enemy in regaining your spiritual equilibrium could be that one word—why.

9. *Allow fun to return to your life.* Grief-stricken and filled with guilt, you find you cannot enjoy life any longer. If you do find yourself having fun, your guilt only increases. You say to yourself—I shouldn't be enjoying myself. I should be covered with sorrow. That may be a normal reaction, but it is very foolish.

God wants you to continue to enjoy life. Jesus said, "I have come so that you might have a more joyful and abundant life." This does not mean that your enjoyment of life stops with the passing of a dear one. You are entitled to your period of grieving, but when it is over you can laugh again. You can take pleasure in the myriad of wonderful things in the world. As you walk into the bright sunshine of a beautiful day and view the clear, blue sky, you hear the birds chirping and the sound of children at play, your heart quickens and the joy of being alive fills your spirit. At this point so many persons will then think, How can I enjoy this day? He or she isn't here to share it.

Put away those thoughts. God created that beautiful day for you to enjoy. It wouldn't be there if He didn't want you to revel in its beauties.

Allow fun to return to your life. Don't shut it out. Don't block it from your life. The one who is gone wouldn't want you to live a joyless life, void of laughter!

10. *If you use your grief—you'll lose your grief.* When you are grief-stricken you find two possibilities open. You will either be drawn closer to God or you will be driven further away. You will become a better person or you will become a worse person. You will become a warmer person or a colder person. You will become a harder person or a softer, gentler, more compassionate person. Your grief has presented these two courses of action. Only *you* have the power to determine what will happen! Use your head—and your heart will follow. Decide that the only reaction that makes any sense is to react positively—not negatively. You owe it to your departed loved one; you owe it to yourself; you owe it to those who are left to live with you. You have no right to indulge in poor selfish grief

and spoil their fun in living. And you owe it to God. He knows, after all, what it is like to lose a Son! His only Son died—you remember—on a cross. Shamefully. Naked. Unfair? Unjust! Too young! What a waste? Yes, these words and more could be raised when you think of Christ dying on a cross. But He used it for good. So can you!

11. *Finally, draw peace from the Christian promise of Eternal Life.* Christ rose from the dead on Easter. That is the Christian claim. I believe it. I believe every last word of it. I believe that this was God's firm and final way of declaring a spiritual truth to comfort his grief-stricken children! "Let not your heart be troubled. You believe in God. Then believe also in me," Jesus said shortly before his own death, adding, "In my father's house are many mansions. *If it were not so I would have told you!"*

I believe in the reliability of Jesus. He said it. I trust him before I trust any doubter or negative thinker.

And now—today—even scientific researchers are affirming the reality of life after death.

New Evidence of Life After Death

The long-standing Christian belief holds to the immortality of the soul. For centuries Christians have claimed that Christ rose from the dead on Easter, and that all people will meet him "on the other side" when our "souls depart from these bodies." Now, at least one noted psychiatrist who has specialized in a study of death and dying has released findings which affirm and virtually "prove" the ancient faith.

Dr. Elizabeth Kubler-Ross is convinced of the continued existence of the psychic life of individuals after biological death.

She specializes in counseling the dying and has studied many deaths, including cases of persons being declared clinically dead but afterward revived. In such cases, she has found, there is always a sense of leaving the body and often of being aware of the efforts of those left behind to resuscitate it. Such persons also describe feeling "peace and wholeness" in death and being met by someone already dead.

She said that she doesn't just believe in life after death, but *knows it to be real.* Her ten years of study have also made her much more religious, she testifies, having been just a "wishy-washy Protestant" when she started.

Her book *On Death and Dying** is described as a standard for those counseling the dying. She feels her studies may help to verify claims of Christianity about life after death.

You can find tremendous power at the deepest center of your being if you can believe the good news that God revealed to the human race through the death and resurrection of Jesus Christ. "He who lives and believes in me shall never die."

Now that you have a way of handling the tension of grief—how do you deal with the petty annoyances?

* New York: Macmillan, Inc., 1969.

VI

Simple Treatments for Common Tensions

"It's not the mountain in the path, but the grain of sand in the shoe that stops many a traveler."

Learn, therefore, how to rid yourself of the daily tensions that trouble the mind, throttle your creative powers, and will contribute more than you know to ill health.

Stress is the root cause of much mental illness. Negative emotions which bring on stress are responsible for many physical ailments as well.

As long ago as 1875 John Ruskin, the art critic and writer, wrote: "The emotions of indignation, grief, controversial anxiety and vanity, or hopeless, and therefore uncontending scorn, are all of them as deadly to the body as poisonous air or polluted water."

Ruskin had been struck by the fact that so many people died in their early fifties, a time at which they could finally become really productive. He must have been able to dismiss those negative tension-producing emotions of which he wrote, from his own mind and soul because he lived a very long and creative life until he died at the age of eighty-two.

In more recent times Canadian researcher Hans Selye has written about the effects of stress or tension on the mind and body. What Ruskin felt instinctively, Selye proved scientifically.

The United States Public Health Service reports that one American in five either has experienced a nervous breakdown or feels himself on the verge of one. It is estimated that one person in every ten is mentally disturbed to the point where some professional treatment is called for.

But you don't have to be one of the five or one of the ten to be under the merciless attack of negative emotions. All of us at one time or another are disturbed by the small inconveniences and interruptions of everyday life.

We know that life is filled with difficulties, problems, petty annoyances, major handicaps, tragedies, and disappointments. We are often unaware that we are on a collision course with some obstacle to happiness or success.

You can find peace of mind as you use Possibility Thinking in the face of little daily tensions.

There are ten basic types of tension that can have devastating effects on our lives. We will identify them and learn some simple ways to meet their challenge.

Do any of these tensions ever cause you difficulty?

1. Inferiority
2. Insecurity
3. Adversity
4. Perplexity
5. Anxiety
6. Irritability
7. Inability
8. Indignity
9. Rigidity
10. Scarcity

Now that you know what they are, it will make it

easier for you to pick those that are causing a blockage of creative thoughts and the achievement of move-ahead goals in your life.

Detect them, and deflect them. Here is how.

1. Find a dynamic possibility thought.
2. Repeat powerful, positive Bible verses.

Now, to cover those Terrible Ten, one by one.

INFERIORITY TENSION

Those who constantly berate themselves for what they believe to be their inadequacies suffer from the tension of inferiority.

This tension-torn soul will often say something like— I'm not intelligent; everybody I come in contact with seems to be much smarter. Or, I haven't accomplished anything in life; I must be a failure. Or, Nobody likes me, or, I'm not very attractive; in fact I'm ugly.

Are you like that? Are you one of those people who constantly tears down himself or herself?

If so, like most people who do this, your opinion of yourself is probably inaccurate. You are better than you think. That's true. Most people are. But how do you come to this realization?

The most important step to take is to understand thoughts of self-condemnation do not come from God. Say to yourself: "I am God's project and God never fails." Let God's love flow into you and fill your life with His presence.

There are vast unrealized and unlimited possibilities within every one of us. You will only discover them if you surrender yourself to the divine plan that God has for your life. Perhaps you have been attempting a career or project that was not meant for you. When you let the power of faith in God enter your life fully and completely you may more easily find your intended role.

Not all of life's successes are determined by business or professional careers. There are many ways in which you can be fulfilled. Your stature as a person is not, and should not be measured by the money you earn or the title on your door. Some of the most successful people in the world have earned their status by serving others.

Remember the story of Gunga Din, the lowly Indian water boy immortalized in Rudyard Kipling's poem. While the British soldiers in India were engaged in fierce fighting under the blazing subtropical sun, Din ran back and forth over the battlefield, carrying cooling water to the men's parched lips. When the faithful Indian was felled by an enemy bullet, the narrator, a tough old soldier, says of him, "You're a better man than I am, Gunga Din."

To help rid yourself of negative, self-deprecating personal criticism, read, memorize, and repeat this healing Bible verse from Psalm 8:

What is man that You art mindful of him and the son of man that You care for him? Yet You have made him a little less than God and You crown him with glory and honor.

Never forget that you are God's idea. And know that God thinks only of great ideas.

INSECURITY TENSION

Feelings of inferiority often produce feelings of insecurity. You know how the insecure person thinks—if he has nothing he starts to believe he will always have nothing.

If he does have material success or possessions he is constantly fearful of losing what he has.

When situations are not going well he grumbles and complains.

When everything falls into place and looks as if it is all going well he thinks, This is too good. It can't last.

He continually concentrates on what he doesn't have instead of looking at what he does have.

Insecurity tension produces a gnawing, self-torturing, permanent state of unhappiness. Insecurity puts you on the defensive and makes you strike out at those around you because of imagined slights. The insecure person may become boastful and try to put other people down. Or he may withdraw, hide and retreat from life's challenges. In either case he becomes nervous, touchy, and pessimistic, shy, depressed, or arrogant.

In turn, this approach to life only serves to reinforce the feelings of inferiority and insecurity. People really do begin to avoid those with aggressive behavior or those who are withdrawn, secretive, and insecure.

Once you realize that God doesn't want you to be unhappy; once you develop a close relationship with your Heavenly Father, slowly but surely, feelings of insecurity will dissolve.

Read, reread, and memorize this powerful Bible verse: "If God be for us who can be against us." (Romans 8:31)

Now relax in the awareness that God loves you and cares about you.

"Cast all your care on Him, for He cares for you." (I Peter 5:7)

The old gospel song tells you that He has the whole world in His hands. You, too, are in His hands.

Affirm daily:

I don't know what tomorrow holds
But I do know who holds tomorrow

ADVERSITY TENSION

Insecurity, if uncorrected, produces adversity. For unsure people quit and give up in the face of trouble. And trouble doesn't become adversity until you allow it to defeat you.

When you are faced with a difficult situation, one that seems insuperable, do you think of quitting?

With adversity tension holding you down you'll find it more difficult than ever to come to grips with problems. Do bear in mind that there *is* a solution to every problem. Reaffirm and repeat the Possibility Thinkers Creed.

> When faced with a mountain,
> I WILL NOT QUIT
> I will keep on striving until I climb over,
> find a pass through, tunnel underneath, or
> simply stay and turn the mountain into
> a gold mine, with God's help.

When adversity threatens—*Handle with Prayer*.

And use this tension-dissolving Bible verse when the going gets rough and you are tempted to quit.

We know that all things work together for good to those that love God and keep His commandments. (Romans 8:28)

Remember that:

Trying Times Are Times to Try More Faith

With greater faith, more prayer, putting greater trust in God, you'll find that trying times will usher in your greatest victories. If you quit, you'll never know what great things you might have accomplished.

Tough times are times for toughness. If you are tough, you'll triumph. The first syllable in the word triumph is *tri (try)*, so never forget—trying times are times to triumph.

PERPLEXITY TENSION

Just about everyone experiences the tension of perplexity, several times during their lifetime. Perplexity is indecision. There are always choices. There is A, B, or C. Or perhaps there is the choice of doing nothing. We face these selections almost every day.

However, there are those persons who are constantly perplexed.

If you have this problem, if you find that perplexity tension prevents you from ever making a firm decision, you will lose the impetus of life. You'll accomplish nothing, achieve nothing. You'll be standing still all your life.

A cartoon published not long ago showed a man seated in his living room before three television sets. Each was tuned to a different channel. In the background his wife was explaining to a visiting neighbor, "That way he doesn't have to make a decision."

That kind of lack of decision-making results in nothing. Nothing positive, nothing constructive, nothing important.

How does one deal with the tension of perplexity? Confidently and quietly, ask God for wisdom and guidance. Trust that He will lead you to make the right decision. He will make clear the course you should take. He will give you the desire and the courage to make the decision that, in His mind, is the right one.

Does this necessarily mean that each decision you make will bring desired results? Not every time. But at least you will have made the decision. In some way every decision you make will prove to be beneficial to you.

As philosopher and educator John Dewey wrote, "The person who really thinks learns quite as much from his failures as from his successes."

Here are your power quotes from the Bible:

In quietness and confidence shall be your strength. (Isaiah 30:15)
Be confident in this one thing that God who has begun a good work in you will complete it. (Philippians 1:6)

Follow this procedure. Think. Pray. Trust. Then, decide without fear. Be confident that you will gain something from every decision but if you make no decision, you are deciding to do nothing.

ANXIETY TENSION

Our century is often referred to as the Age of Anxiety. Almost everyone is anxious about something. Adults are very concerned about the behavior of the younger generation. Young people are fearful about the future of the human race. And anxiety is one of the best (or worst) tension producers of all.

Much of our anxiety is caused by scare headlines in newspapers and the general tone of news reporting on the radio, over television, as well as in the press. Charles L. Gould, publisher of the San Francisco *Examiner*, once compiled a list of some of the positive aspects of life. It would be a rarity if any of the following facts from Mr. Gould's list ever made a newspaper headline.

In the present year:

More than 196,000,000 of our people will not be arrested.

More than 89,000,000 married people will not file for divorce.

More than 115,000,000 individuals will maintain a formal affiliation with some religious group.

More than 75,000,000 citizens and corporations will pay more than $160 billion in income taxes.

More than 4,000,000 teachers, preachers, and professional people will not strike or participate in riotous demonstrations.

A great deal of anxiety tension can be dispelled if we look at the positive aspects of life. That applies not only to the over-all view of the nation and the world, but also to our personal life. No matter how many problems you may have, if you think about your life you'll find many uplifting, positive areas. Concentrate on what you have, not on what you have not.

Poverty is certainly not to be desired but, along with other observers, I have noted that many poor families are happier than some of those with great wealth.

Some physically handicapped persons lead more joyous lives than others who are in perfect health. Joni Erickson is a paraplegic and has lost the use of her arms and legs, yet she paints beautiful pictures using her teeth to hold the brush. And I know of few people who are so happily infused with the joy of the Lord as she is.

How do you go about curing anxiety tension? The search by individuals for a cure for this malady is more widespread today than ever before. There are many kinds of therapy and systems being touted these days which purport to remove the anxieties of life. There are logotherapy, reality therapy, milieu therapy, among others. There is also transactional analysis, motivational therapy, and much more.

However, no system of therapy has ever proved more successful in dissolving tensions than the kind of faith in God demonstrated by Jesus Christ. Read the healing word of Jesus, the world's greatest possibility thinker.

And which of you by being anxious can add one cubit to his span of life. (Matthew 6:27)
Ask and you shall receive.
Seek and you shall find.
Knock and it shall be opened to you. (Matthew 7:7)

IRRITABILITY TENSION

There are so many things happening in the world that irritate and exasperate us it is no wonder that irritability-causing tension is found in profusion. So much goes wrong. So many things are done imperfectly or discourteously.

There is the tailgater on the highway or the speedster or the horn honker. There are the inexperienced sales-clerks unfamiliar with their merchandise. How about the plumber who turns up on Thursday instead of Wednesday? The husband who is caught in homebound traffic and ruins a special dinner? And the errors on store computers and bank statements? Yes, there are a thousand and one small abrasive situations that arise as we go through life.

Of course, becoming irritated solves nothing. It doesn't improve matters or even remove the cause. If we are upset and irritated it only means one more roadblock to serenity and constructive living has been created. Remember the actor in many, many movies who would become so distressed by some event that he would take his hat off and stomp on it only to look at it in disgust. His irritability had caused him to destroy something he wanted and needed. In a real sense that is what we do when we become distressed over a small incident. We destroy our creative powers by blocking them with the tension of irritability.

Like most people, I've had my share of irritable moments. Most of the time I can rise above this kind of tension with the help of these three prescriptions.

The first is a Bible verse—"Fret not yourself because of problem people. Trust in the Lord and do good." (Psalms 37:1)

Next comes a possibility thought: *Every irritation is an invitation to an elevation.*

What does this mean? Simply that when you are irritated you can turn that into an opportunity to rise higher, above the petty inconveniences of the world, and become a bigger and better person. When you are frustrated by the inconsiderate actions of another person you can rise above it. You have a chance to demonstrate true patience, tolerance and understanding. The world will be a better place for seeing this kind of Christ-love in action.

Thirdly, I keep remembering the story about a crabby old woman seated on a bus in Chicago who was making a fuss. She was complaining about her fellow passengers, the swaying of the bus, the conversation of two people nearby, and generally making loud and disconcerting comments. As she was about to leave a gentleman seated across the way said, "Just a minute, ma'am. You left something behind." Startled, she asked, "What?" The kindly fellow replied, "A very bad impression."

Stated otherwise: Every irritation is an opportunity to leave a good impression behind.

INABILITY TENSION

Inability tension arises when you get the horrible feeling of being unable to cope with everyday and usually familiar situations. It's when you seem unable to perform tasks that other persons of like intelligence and ability are tackling and succeeding at. Sometimes it occurs when you find you can't complete a job that you had managed so easily in the past.

Inability tension is not caused by a lack of ability. You have the ability but it is being blocked. Somehow you have developed the personality of an impossibility thinker. Affirm aloud the Possibility Thinkers Creed over and over again to start you on the road to overcoming your problem.

> When faced with a mountain,
> I WILL NOT QUIT
> I will keep on striving until I climb over,
> find a pass through, tunnel underneath, or
> simply stay and turn the mountain into
> a gold mine, with God's help.

Affirm:

> Whatever the Mind Can Believe
> The Human Being Can Achieve

It was all best expressed by Jesus when He said, "All things are possible to him who believes." Keep repeating this powerful message which comes to you from God.

INDIGNITY TENSION

Nothing is more torturous than having indignities heaped upon you. The most inhuman act a person can inflict upon a fellow member of the human race is to deliberately and purposefully insult him or her. The heaping of indignities, insults, and injustices upon others caused Jesus to condemn in the strongest language those who acted and spoke as "holier than thou's."

Self-respect, self-worth, self-dignity, these are your birthrights. When self-worth is assaulted, when self-respect is attacked, when self-dignity is undermined, a justly conceived but terribly self-destructive resentment is generated. The tension that results can provoke a wonderful person to violence and always causes a blockage of productive energies.

We see this happening among members of minority groups. In the United States these are the blacks, the Hispanics, the Mexican-Americans, the Jews, and in some areas Catholics. In other countries Protestants, Catholics, Mohammedans, and other religious factions are subjected to the same brand of indignities and insults.

The tension of indignity is created in other areas and situations. Women are mistreated by some men who constantly speak and act in insulting ways. Too often business executives fail to respect the dignity of their workers, and individuals at the top of the social ladder look down at those they consider inferior.

How do you deal with the stress brought about when you are on the receiving end of such indignities?

The answer lies in the wisdom given in the words of Jesus Christ, "If any one strikes you on the right cheek, turn to him the other also." The meaning of these words sometimes eludes readers. It is precisely in dealing with the problem of indignity tension that their meaning becomes crystal clear. They reveal a fantastic insight by Jesus in learning how to meet the challenge of the insult.

What He is telling us here is that the person innocent of any wrongdoing who is degraded must not let his treatment at the hands of another get under his skin.

If you don't "turn the other cheek" and you let the insult get to you, a problem of immeasurable duration, effect, and intensity will result. You will be choked by resentment, and hostility produced by your negative overreaction to the insult will be far more damaging and destructive to you than the insult itself.

But how do you prevent this overreaction on your part? First remind yourself that almost everyone, no matter of what race, religion, color, or social position, is put down at one time or another. It is not a unique experience. It is the price we pay for living in an overcrowded society.

The next step is for you to use the positive power of possibility thinking toward the person who insulted you. *He* has a problem. Why? Is he ignorant, prejudiced, or does he just have an unkind disposition? What negative emotions are surging through him? Perhaps he has been goaded into this action by physical pain or mental illness or family problems. In any case he has a bigger problem than you *unless you let the hurt dominate your emotions*. He is more to be pitied than censured. He needs your prayers.

Always remember:

> What happens to you
> Isn't as important
> As your reaction to
> What happens to you.

RIGIDITY TENSION

This stiff, unbending tension is found in those who are rigid in their beliefs and opinions and uncompromising about the ideas and attitudes of others. In a certain sense the development of this type of tension has been aided and abetted by some religious leaders. Such clergymen under the protection of the authority-umbrella of being ministers of God sometimes produce their own rules, touting them as God-made dictums. They then proceed to superimpose these rules on their followers, and further inform their followers that they will be good Christians only by obeying these man-made rules along with the threat of spiritual punishment for violating them.

I am not talking about basic religious and ethical standards such as the Ten Commandments. We cannot compromise with them.

Parents who are rigid in their thinking and treat their offspring as if they were committing a sin for differing with them create what is generally known as the generation gap. Rigidity tension in parents prevents the full expression of love and devotion that family life should engender.

I am proud that my wife and I have not experienced a generation gap with our children. Mrs. Schuller and I have always conveyed and communicated to our five children our religious convictions and our moral principles. We live by these principles at home as well as in public life. We strongly believe that if we live according to a specific moral code our children will accept it. This has proven successful.

At the same time, since our children are individuals on their own, we respect each one's right to be his or her own person.

The freedom to be different and individual under God is one of God's greatest gifts. Respect each person's individuality and appreciate the fact that no two are exactly alike. Otherwise the tension of rigidity will set in to strangle your mind.

Bend to the other person's viewpoint. You don't have to accept it, but try to understand and be tolerant of those who think differently than you. You'll then stay free of rigidity tension and you may well learn something new. Open your own mind to the thoughts of others.

Our church building has a long wall made of sliding glass doors. It's a beautiful sight to behold. Not too long after the church was built there was a strong windstorm. As the wind pressed steadily against the huge glass windows the wall began to billow in like a ship's sail. Anticipating a crescendo of the sound of broken glass, I hurriedly called our architect, Richard Neutra.

In an excited voice I reported, "The walls in the church are bending. They'll cave in any minute. I think you should have used sturdier framing material."

To my surprise, he chuckled as he began to assure me and restore my confidence. "Don't worry; we designed those frames to bend under extreme wind pressure. If they bend, they won't break. If we had made them as rigid as you suggest they wouldn't be able to bend and the sheets of glass would break or blow out."

Over the next fifteen years I observed that many rigid store-front windows have blown out in various windstorms whereas our flexibly framed sliding glass doors have survived unbroken.

Bend a Little or End Up Brittle

is a fundamental principle for tensionless living.

112

To further relieve rigidity tension use this Bible verse, the words of Jesus Christ:

Judge not, that you be not judged. (Matthew 7:1)

SCARCITY-OF-TIME TENSION

A major cause of nerve-wrecking tension is the seeming shortage of time. Too many people try to handle this problem in one of two ways—either of which only aggravates the situation. One way is to overwork, using night and day and weekends in order to meet the scheduled deadline. The second solution is to delay the deadline and be late in completing whatever it is you are involved in.

Both methods result in a vicious cycle of fatigue and weariness, fighting the pressures of deadlines and producing a stress on your physical and emotional health that brings only more difficulties.

To reduce the scarcity-of-time tension I have found it necessary to adopt this simple procedure:

Plan ahead; when you fail to plan, you are planning to fail.

I am frequently asked how I find time to write books, lecture across the United States, direct a television ministry, plus build a church (and now a crystal cathedral), and still go out to personally raise the millions of dollars needed to sustain this work. The answer is simple.

1. I constantly review my goals, reorganize my priorities, and update my commitments. So I keep putting first things first—which means I cut out of my life today certain functions that "I no longer have time for because larger challenges command my time today."

2. Now I determine what I need to do to reach the updated objectives and I rearrange my calendar accordingly.

3. Now I write my plans on the calendar which then manages and controls my life! It's really so very, very simple.

SCARCITY-OF-MONEY TENSION

What about the tension brought about by the scarcity of money?

Realize that few people have money problems—almost always it's a management problem. I had breakfast not too long ago with a wealthy friend. He is an intimate friend of the members of one of America's most renowned super-rich families. "They have an income of $800,000 a year," he reported, "but they always are short on cash."

"How can that be?" I protested.

"You can't imagine how they live," he explained. "Four homes, all huge estates, the taxes, maintenance, insurance, and help are eating it up!"

By contrast I know of a young bachelor who lives very comfortably in Los Angeles on three thousand dollars a year. He budgets thirty dollars a week for food and necessities. He lives in a small but comfortable apartment. He buys his food at discount prices. He buys day-old bread. He's a writer and is very happy.

My mother, until her death not many years ago, also lived on an annual income of less than three thousand dollars a year.

Cultivate the lost art of management. Eliminate waste.

Having followed this plan, which will help you move up the ladder and prosper, it is important to keep always in the forefront of your mind the fact that God wants you to prosper. Read and repeat this Bible verse:

He who sows sparingly will also reap sparingly, and he who sows bountifully will also reap bountifully. (II Corinthians 9:6)

To that add the words of Jesus Christ:

I am come that you might have life and have it more abundantly. (John 10:10)

And very importantly:

Give and it shall be given unto you.

The above verses contain the secret of financial security.

Give generously to build God's dream and God will give back more than you ever expected. Give of your time or a portion of your worldly goods no matter how little they may be. You'll be amazed at what happens. But it does.

Build a Dream and the Dream Will Build You

The secret of success is simple—find a need and fill it. Find a hurt and heal it. Find a problem and solve it. Find an obstacle and remove it. And those who are deeply helped will be so grateful they'll thank you with an expression of love that will astound you.

You will be able to face your future with deep inner security. What you must do now is erase all fear and worry from your mind and face tomorrow with quiet hope.

VII

Six Steps to Rid Yourself of Fear and Worry

Fear and worry are two of the greatest tension builders of all time. To succeed in turning tension off and turning power on, it is absolutely imperative that we eliminate worry and fear.

It's possible—to be rid of worry and fear
It's possible—to have peace of mind
It's possible—if you take these six positive steps to:

Bury Your Worry and Clear Out Fear

1. *Face them.* Face your worries. Don't avoid them. With God's all-powerful help you will be in top condition to handle your worries. However, before you can erase them you have to face them.

Nothing in the Bible encourages us to seek cowardly escape from worry. God does not teach us to run from the fears of life. If you try to run from them, they'll master you. So much of the frenetic, fitful, pleasure seeking of our times is a frantic attempt by some people to avoid facing head on a worrisome situation.

You'll be amazed when you discover how worries disappear when you bring them out in the open. Talk about them with friends or with those who may be able to help in doing something about them.

Ralph Waldo Emerson wrote, "Do the thing you fear and the death of fear is certain."

Repeat the words of Isaiah, "Fear not for I am with you." (43:5)

In his book *Stay Alive All Your Life*† Dr. Norman Vincent Peale writes:

> Picture yourself boldly attacking and overcoming your fears . . . boldness will reveal to you that you are stronger than you have imagined. Fear will diminish and courage rise in direct proportion to the effectiveness with which you put boldness into effect. Practice first the bold thought and, second, the bold act. This will stimulate supporting spiritual forces that will enable you to overcome fear.

In the same book, Dr. Peale tells how his friend, author Arthur Gordon, wrote:

> I was facing a decision that involved considerable risk. I took the problem to a friend much older and wiser than myself. "I'd go ahead," I said unhappily, "if I were sure I could swing it but . . ." He looked at me for a moment, then scribbled ten words on a piece of paper and pushed it across the desk. I picked it up and read, in a single sentence, the best advice I ever had:

> *Be Bold and Mighty Forces Will Come to Your Aid*

Your worries will flee like ghostly shadows when the light is turned on, if you will only face them. Enormous

† New York: Prentice-Hall, 1957.

courage will rise within you as you realize that with God you can face anything.

2. *Trace them.* The second step in liberating yourself from the grip of fear and worry is to analyze the causes of your anxieties. Track the culprit down. Look for the real underlying cause of your apprehensions. In doing this you will often find that expert psychological counseling can be very helpful.

One troubled woman took her worrisome mental miseries to the counseling center at the Tower of Hope. Our psychologist quickly traced her problems to their roots. Suffering from an inferiority complex she was terribly concerned that her husband was being unfaithful. With the revelation of the origins of her worry, she was able to be guided to a new wholesome self-confidence. When she began to look upon herself as a beautiful person, she started to banish her fears from her life.

Here is the kind of situation that is very familiar to just about every pastor and psychological counselor and every psychiatrist. The person who is consulting the expert explains that he is troubled; he is worried and apprehensive about his daily life. He says that he is mysteriously anxious about the future although he cannot pinpoint anything specific. In this situation the psychiatrist, psychologist, or pastoral counselor will try to bring out what is at the bottom of all this anxiety. Most often the culprit is revealed as the demon we know as "guilt."

Guilt can be removed. If the counselor is aware of the healing powers of Jesus Christ, the forgiveness of the Lord, and the blessings of God, the patient will, in accepting these gifts, find his guilt removed.

If any man be in Christ he is a new creature, old things are passed away.

3. *Place them.* Now—put your worries in their proper perspective—in their place in your life. Many worries that dominate your mind should be relegated or demoted to the minor position they really should occupy. Man has an enormous capacity to exaggerate. One man asked me, "You say I can move mountains. How can I move my mountain?"

After analyzing his problem, I said, "You don't face a mountain; you face a molehill."

In order to put your problem into its proper perspective, ask yourself how important it will appear a year from now. What difference will it make in your life in ten years? Is it a matter of money, of personal relationships, of business, or is it really a matter of life and death? Does your life depend on it?

If it seems to be a really serious situation, give the matter your most earnest prayers and attention.

In so many cases, after you've put the situation in its proper place, the fears subside and new confidence replaces them. We permit ourselves to become overly concerned about too many insignificant and unessential situations in our complex and confused life.

We often concern ourselves with contingencies that are so remote that it is ridiculous for us even to consider them. This is well illustrated in the following situation paraphrased from Lewis Carroll's *Through the Looking-Glass:* Alice encounters the White Knight, sitting on his white horse. He's carrying a beehive, and she asks, "What are you carrying a beehive for?" "Well," he says, "I may, in my travels, run into a swarm of bees, and if I do I can catch them in here." He had a big collection of mousetraps and she questions, "What are you doing with the mousetraps?" He says, "Well, I may just run into some mice, and if I do I can catch them, you see." "But, what are all those knives around the feet of your horse for?" she queries. "Well, I expect that I may be traveling through some waters and if I run into sharks, the knives on the feet of my horse will ward the sharks off," he answers.

One of the secrets of happy living is to "travel light." Unload those unnecessary worries. They are only excess baggage. Identify the really important items and eliminate the insignificant, the inconsequential, and the marginal.

After that, place your worries in the right department. When we first started our church it was in a drive-in theater completely open to the elements. Every Saturday night I used to worry about whether or not it would rain the following day. Finally it dawned on me that I couldn't do anything about the weather. I told myself, "It's not your department, Schuller, it's not your responsibility."

It is really amazing how many of our concerns and worries are really God's responsibility.

When Oliver Cromwell was the ruler of England he sent his secretary on an important mission, to deliver a vital message to a key political figure on the Continent. The secretary was carefully instructed by Cromwell as to the exact time, and the exact way he was to present the message, even to the exact tone of voice he was to use.

With a close companion accompanying him, Cromwell's secretary took the boat to cross the English Channel. All night long he tossed and turned in his bed. His companion, noting this, asked what was wrong. The secretary replied that he felt he was not going to be able to accomplish the mission successfully, that he would be unable to fulfill his responsibility.

The companion asked him, "Do you believe that before you and Oliver Cromwell were born that God ruled the world?"

The answer in the darkened stateroom was, "Of course."

Then, "Do you believe, sir, that after you and Cromwell are gone that God will still rule the world?"

"Indeed, I do," was the reply.

"Do you believe that God is ruling today?"

Giving another affirmative answer, peace came into the courier's mind.

Yes, God is there and, when you are fearful, put your faith in His divine guidance.

4. *Space them.* You should now develop the skill of spacing your problems. Don't jam them all into your mind at the same time.

I recall a counseling session with a person who was filled with fears. They covered the past, the present, and the future. There were too many for any human mind to deal with. "Put plenty of space between your worries," I advised.

"Yesterday is past. Forget it. Tomorrow is in the future. Let's just deal with the next five minutes. Can you face the next five minutes without worry, the next ten minutes, the next hour, the entire day?"

If so, that's all you need to face.

A man who had read the autobiography of the controversial French author Colette met her and said, "I noticed that when you were a teen-ager, and in your early twenties, you seemed to have had a very happy life."

"Yes," she answered. "It's too bad I didn't realize it at the time."

This is so true for most of us as we look back upon our past years. We were so happy then. Why didn't we enjoy them more? Usually because we were busy borrowing tomorrow's fears, worries, and anxieties.

All you have is today. Enjoy it. Today is filled with God. Today is filled with beauty. Enjoy the present. Don't allow tomorrow's fears to blot out today's joy.

Here is a prayer which I think expresses these thoughts:

> Lord, for tomorrow and its needs, I do not pray.
> Keep me from stain of sin just for today.
> Help me to labor earnestly and duly pray.
> Let me be kind in word and deed, Father, today.
> Let me no idle word unthinking say.
> Set thou a seal upon my lips through all today.
> Let me in season, Lord, be grave; in season, gay.
> Let me be faithful to thy grace, O Lord, today.
> And if today this life of mine should ebb away,
> Give me thy sacrament divine, Father, I pray.
> So, for tomorrow and its needs I do not pray.
> Just keep me, guide me, love me, Lord, through each today.

Use this prayer and you'll find many of your worries and fears vanishing. This will happen if you believe that you and God have things under control, that you will live one day at a time.

Give us this day, *this* day, our daily bread.

Remember to space your worries. Ask yourself what the one important matter is that you should concern yourself about today. Blot out the others. Then tackle that one concern with all you've got.

Be not concerned about tomorrow:

The morrow will take thought for itself.

Sufficient unto the day is the worry thereof. (Matthew 6:34)

A wise pastor, confronted by a troubled parishioner, pointed to the traffic flowing over a nearby bridge and said, "Do you realize how much weight that bridge carries in a month or a year? It does it by taking a few cars at a time. It would collapse if it didn't carefully ration its load."

You'll find enormous peace of mind when you space your worries.

Trust God and Live One Day at a Time

5. *Grace them.* See if you can turn your hostile worries into gracious friends.

G. Wallace Hamilton tells of seeing a young Arab in North Africa playing a flute. Looking closely he discovered that the musical instrument had been made from an old rifle left over from World War II. Someone had drilled holes in the barrel and turned the instrument of death into an instrument of pleasure.

Try to bestow grace on your concerns. Look upon them as being potential blessings in disguise. Perhaps you can use your worries, fears, and apprehensions to motivate you to become a better person.

When your worries motivate you into tackling some undisciplined area of your life with a burst of determination to improve yourself—that is crowning your worries with grace and glory.

Worry can be a gift of God's grace if it frightens you into quitting a habit that could destroy you. It can be a gift of God if it alarms you into breaking off a relationship that could be dangerous. It can be a gift of God if it concerns you over a lack of funds and energizes you into working with vigor and enthusiasm.

Let your fears and worries turn you to prayer, to church, to God. Turn the destructive, negative rifle barrels in your life into positive instruments of joy and accomplishment.

6. *Erase your worries*. Now, it is time to erase those worries that cannot be turned into positive motivating forces.

Let the hand and spirit of Jesus Christ move across your mind to erase worry and fear just as an eraser moves across a blackboard and eliminates words written with chalk.

Peace I leave with you, My peace I give unto you.

Vague worry; nameless tension; that inner feeling of discontent that defies description. What is it? How does it come about? Sociologists, anthropologists, psychologists have probed the problem and have come up with some answers. But no answer that ignores man's spiritual nature is total and complete. No person who overlooks God can completely help you quiet the trembling, quivering, disquieting apprehension deep in your soul. By nature man is instinctively spiritual and religious.

The nameless, gnawing, stubborn apprehension that eats away at you is your soul longing to go home again. And God is the homeland of the soul.

As I write these words I am in my studio overlooking the Pacific Ocean. There is a school of great California gray whales swimming north. Two months before I had seen them heading south to Baja, California, where the cows deliver their young in the warm waters off Mexico. Now they are headed homeward, to Alaskan waters, their true home.

Perhaps it is my imagination, but they seem to be happier, more playful as they head toward home. These great whales, flapping their large flat tails, slapping the Pacific, seem to be glad to be going home to the crisp, cool Arctic. With powerful surges of energy they plunge ahead, their hulking bodies humping through the sea, driven by this instinctive, insatiable urge to return to their homeland.

So it is with you. There is a drive within us to return to God.

At some time in the past, you may have taken a turn on the road of life. Perhaps that turn took you in a different direction, away from your ancestral homeland, further and further away from God.

Perhaps you had new and exciting experiences. There was fresh scenery, new sights and sounds, new sensations. You tasted new drinks, tried new pleasures, sang new songs, and danced new dances. It was gay, exciting—a swinging new life.

All of this new-found pleasure wiped out of your consciousness the boring recollection of your old homeland, that backward world that really wasn't with it.

Now, the new thrills have worn off. There is an aftertaste on your tongue. After the initial sweetness comes the touch of bitterness that often follows the sweetness of saccharine. The high life doesn't give you the kicks it once did. You are like a traveler on the road, living out of a suitcase. You are eager to return home. You are eager for the honest faces, the way common people have of looking you in the eye without blinking.

Now you know you are homesick. There is that mysterious longing, that disturbing mood. Soon you see it for what it is. It is your soul, homesick for God. God is calling you home again.

The feeling grows stronger and stronger. It is like the mood of a wild stallion prancing in his corral, his ears attuned to the air waves to catch a distant, faint call from the hills; his nostrils open wide to pick up a wisp of a scent that drifts down on a stray wind. Something deep within his being tells him he doesn't belong in this box made of fences. He runs restlessly around the yard, cutting to the far side where he turns gracefully, arches his neck, picks up his hoofs, breaks suddenly into a mad gallop and in one beautiful expression of muscle power leaps, soars, and catapults over the fence. With mane and tail flying in the wind he races across the plains, heading for the hills and his homeland. At last he is free.

Yes, that is the feeling you'll have when you sense the call of God pulling you back to your homeland, giving you the strength to soar over the confining fences of daily fears and worries.

You will find faith again. You will rejoice in your faith. You will be free at last.

VIII

Meditate Your Way to Quiet Power

You are ready, now, to discover and develop the tranquillity-inducing experience of meditation. To handle all of the tensions we have discussed thus far, including hurts, grief, worry, and fear, you can use the time-tested technique called meditation for deep peace of mind. In one form or another, meditation has been practiced, for centuries and millenniums, by adherents of almost every religion.

In recent years it has been scientifically proven through experiments and measurements that man's conscious mind can control bodily functions that were previously thought to be completely involuntary. Natural processes like the rate of breathing, the heartbeat, metabolic rate, even the pattern of brain waves can be affected and slowed down by the process of meditation.

It strikes me as being ironic that what the Bible has been saying for four to five thousand years in the Old Testament and for two thousand years in the New Testament is now being accepted because it has been scientifically and medically proven. It has taken electrical measurements, electrodes on the body, the charts of encephalograms and electrocardiograms, to convince modern man of the efficacy of the Bible and the word of God.

Dr. Herbert Benson is only one of the physicians who

have confirmed the reality of meditation power. His book, *The Relaxation Response,* affirms beyond a shadow of a doubt the integrity and reality of the principles of meditation.

Dr. Barbara Brown of the University of California was among the first to make these discoveries. Prior to her work it was assumed that human beings live on one of three levels of consciousness: (1) the state of being awake, (2) the state of being asleep and (3) the hypnotic state. Dr. Brown's discovery was a fourth and very distinct state now commonly called the "Alpha state." Actually it is now assumed there may be many other levels of consciousness that have yet to be analyzed, labeled, and understood. It is the Alpha state with which we are now concerned.

The Alpha state is one of deep tranquillity. The mind is blank. It is drained of all conscious thought. It occurs in deep meditation. I like to think of this as being medication meditation. It is medication for your spirit. It cleanses you. Remember:

MEDITATION IS MEDICATION

"Biofeedback" is the word Dr. Brown coined to describe the physical body's reactions to the Alpha state. Modern biofeedback machines have found their way into psychiatrists' offices. Like lie-detector machines, and heart-monitoring machines, biofeedback machines pick up the blood pressure, skin temperature, and heartbeat. A graph with a swinging needle shows instantly to the person being tested, his state of consciousness and body reaction. I myself have been "hooked up" to the expensive biofeedback machine from the office of a Christian psychiatrist in California. The registered nurse, Mrs. Donald Brandt, an epert in this field, monitored the machine as I went into meditation. "Good! Great! Possibility Thinking Meditation really works for you!" she said as I quickly responded. "And if Possibility Thinking Meditation (PTM) works for you it can work for others," she enthused.

A variety of approaches to meditation as a technique for achieving release from tension and stress is employed by many different religions as well as by various non-religious mind-control systems. In all forms of meditation, however, there is one similar aspect, whether the form or system is TM, Zen Buddhism, or Yoga or one of the many methods of meditation developed through the five thousand years of Judaeo-Christian tradition. In it the meditator endeavors to overcome the distractions of the conscious mind.

In some forms of meditation you are instructed to focus on a particular object or image. It may be turning your eyes inward so that you can see the tip of your nose. In some cases you are asked to visualize an eye near the top of the back of your head. The monks in their monasteries would focus their eyes on a crucifix.

Likewise, the mantra, or chant, a device employed in many forms of Eastern meditation serves to distract the subconscious from tension-producing stimuli. A mantra is not mystic. It is a group of sounds designed to be repeated over and over again in order to remove the distractions of the material world.

The most effective mantras employ the "M" sound. You can get the feel of it by repeating the words, "I am. I am," many times over. The vibrating hum mounts from your lips through your head to the vicinity of your brain. The vibrations relax the mind even as a vibrating barber chair or vibrating bed relaxes muscles.

The "mantra" has been and is being widely discussed through the advocates of one of the most successfully merchandised forms of meditation. I refer to Transcendental Meditation or TM, as it is commonly called. It is not a religion nor is it necessarily anti-Christian. It is, however, commercially non-Christian. It does not integrate into its practice the dynamic love and positive power of Jesus Christ. For this reason I advocate the Meditation that Christ practiced. I call it: PTM, or Possibility Thinking Meditation.

PTM is not new. It is older than Christ Himself. Dr. Herbert Benson in *Relaxation Response* reveals there is built in every person a "capacitor" which, triggered by meditation turns tension off and turns peace of mind on.

In a very revealing interview in *Book Digest* the following dialogue with a Harvard doctor takes place:

Q. "How did previous generations trigger the relaxation response?"

A. "By prayer and meditation."

It is important to remember that meditation in any form is the harnessing, by human beings, of God's divine laws. God created humans differently from all other creatures on the face of the earth. He created within us a conscious and a subconscious mind. We are endowed with a great many powers and forces that we do not yet fully understand. He meant us to use our minds, our emotions, and our powers in constructive, creative, and positive ways, in order to achieve peace of mind, fulfillment, accomplishment, and joyous, harmonious life.

The Purpose of PTM

Each discipline that seeks to open the road to meditation aims at a different although somewhat similar state

132

of being. In TM it is to achieve a condition of rest, a blankness. In Zen Buddhism it is described as a black blank. Yoga sets forth as its goal the awareness of a universal spiritual giver.

The aim of what I like to call Possibility Thinking Meditation is to rest in the Lord and to wait patiently for Him. In PTM we do not aim to reach the Alpha state simply for the purpose of lowering the blood pressure—important though that is.

The purpose of PTM is to reach the state of relaxation where you can be released from negative tensions that block the possible flow of creative ideas—even the very voice and Spirit of God! "Be still and know that I am God." Remember the theme of this book, "tranquillity is conditioning for communication."

I am often asked the difference between PTM (Possibility Thinking Meditation) and TM (Transcendental Meditation). The difference is Jesus Christ. He is my God-sent Guru. And there is no argument here: *Any person, even an atheist, will change if he allows the teaching, the spirit and the example of Christ to inspire him. Any person will become a better person if he becomes a follower of Christ. For he inspires us to be unselfish.*

Meaningless mantras repeated over and over will never be as effective as Christian meditation which brings Jesus Christ's love into our daily lives. For the love of Jesus Christ is unequaled in its ability to produce peace at a very deep level. When you meditate as a Christian you focus on Him. You don't need another guru if you have Jesus Christ in your life. Join me then in becoming a PTM, Possibility Thinking Meditator.

Five Steps to Effective Meditation

1. *Neutralize your mind.* In order to meditate effectively, you begin by relaxing, slowing down your fast-moving conscious mind, in effect throwing your mental gears into neutral. It's a little like putting the gearshift of a car in the neutral position. You turn off the fast, forward-moving thinking, and take your mental activity out of reverse gear. In other words stop thinking about what you have done, or have not done, or will be doing. Throw your conscious mind in neutral. Imagine your brain in neutral, simply and quietly purring and humming, concentrating on nothing but the soft, quiet, neutralizing vibrating mental hum.

To help achieve this state of mind relax the muscles of your body. Sit in a comfortable chair. Feel your weight resting on the chair. Now feel yourself growing lighter—almost floating. Close your eyes and keep them closed through the several steps of meditation. Your closed eyes will eliminate the possibility of visual distractions that would throw your mind in gear again.

2. *Harmonize.* Remember, the purpose of PTM is to achieve a oneness of spirit with God—the Eternal Creative Intelligence. Harmony with His spirit is essential to be deeply effective. Hear the instructions of a great meditator, the Psalmist of the Bible:

"Let the words of my mouth and the meditations of my heart be acceptable in thy sight, O Lord, my strength and my Redeemer." (Psalms 19:14)

Concentrate on these Bible verses, "not my will but your will be done, Lord." "Peace I leave with you, my peace I give unto you."

Life Changing, Power Generating, Possibility Thinking Meditation is a duet not a solo. Even though you throw your conscious mind in neutral you wait—you listen with the *attitude* of *harmonizing your will* with the Creator's perfect holy will.

After all, the positive purpose of PTM is to become the person God wants you to be. You are in quietness prepared to adjust your thoughts to tune in to His beautiful wave length. And when you tune in to His will you tune in to peace.

If you drive an automobile you know that every once in a while when your car is in for servicing, you will be told that the wheels are out of alignment. This causes the tires to wear unevenly. The outer or inner walls of the tires become worn to the point of being dangerous. The service manager will suggest that you have your wheels realigned.

In a similar way that's what PTM is all about. In PTM you don't have a wheel alignment but a *will* alignment. If your nerves are wearing thin you need a will alignment.

You line up your mind with God. You achieve deep, inner harmony and when you finish meditating you will be energized and vitalized and able to get the maximum mileage out of your life!

Harmony is when two or more persons listen to each other. In PTM your heart listens to God's silent spirit and He listens to your silent spirit. A harmony of spiritual silence is the beautiful result.

3. *Sterilize.* Out of the deep silence an unsettling feeling may surface. Like an oil stain rising from the deep to swirl and float in clear view, deep-seated negative emotions may emerge—perhaps some resentment, jealousy, guilt, or hidden hurt. Neither make a conscious effort to dredge them from your subconscious, nor seek to repress them if they naturally appear. Allow

135

God, the ultimate healing force of forgiving peace, to bring them out—if He chooses. As they come in focus on the neutralized and God-harmonized screen of your meditating mind believe and be sure that your awareness and consciousness of them is the proof that God is now in the process of removing them from your life. This is His process of spiritually sterilizing, purifying, and cleansing your soul of an accumulation of emotionally polluting experiences that have been the source of inner tensions. Relax and allow God's cleansing spirit to draw out the poisons. Feel the fresh air of His purifying spirit flowing in. When you complete your moments of PTM you will open your eyes and feel cleansed! Purified! Renewed! Forgiven! Saved! Born Again!

4. *Tranquillize.* Now release—let go any unsettling, disturbing memories or moods that come to your mind. You are willing, and unconditionally committed to permanently forget selfish hurts, harbored resentments, or foolish jealousies.

Picture a quiet pool of water. In your mind see naughty boys approach. They strike the peaceful surface with sticks, churning and troubling the water. Now they leave and run off carrying their disturbing sticks with them. And the water settles down from angry churning to ripples, to gentle undulating and mirrored unmoving calm. What the peace-disturbing sticks in the hands of naughty boys is in relation to the waters—that is what negative memories and bad feelings are to your peace of mind. Let them go like naughty boys and let peace return to your mind.

It may help you to concentrate on Christ's healing words. If you feel you would benefit from a "mantra" take the "I am's" of Jesus Christ and repeat them softly, chanting, humming, affirming His presence and peace within you as you recite His promises.

"I am the way, the truth and the Life. No one comes to the Father but by me."

"I am the resurrection and the Life. He who lives and believes in me shall never die."

"I am the door: by me if any one enter, he shall be saved."

Believe He is the Eternal Christ—Eternal Love—Eternal Peace—is within you now as you repeat over and over and over and over the words "I am" "I am" "I am" "I am" "I am."

5. *Visualize.* To bring beautiful peace to your mind, and experience the strokes of serenity across your spirit, move your mind now to meditate on peaceful scenes.

For a general meditation simply visualize a beautiful picture. A quiet lake with gentle waves, weeping willow trees with branches that almost touch the water.

Special Meditation for Specific Tensions

Now learn to use PTM to find release and relief from specific tensions.

WHEN YOU FEEL DEPRESSED

Sit in a comfortable upholstered chair, one that enables you to feel perfectly relaxed. Rest your head against the back of the chair and place your hands on the arms. Now close your eyes.

Use your imagination. Visualize yourself rising up, up, up through the ceiling, up through the roof of your house until you are floating over neighboring rooftops. You are high above the noisy hum of traffic in the streets below. As you float higher and higher the roar of the traffic, the honking of horns, the shouts of motorists—all recede in the distance. All you can hear is the soft whisper of clouds as they pass by. Serenity surrounds you as you float through the azure blue sky.

You continue to rise higher and higher. You are weightless, almost like a feather as you drift through the air. Finally you are in outer space. You can no longer see houses or people or cars. Beneath you, the earth is just a large round ball. Only oceans and continents are visible. You see what the astronauts see on their trips to the moon. You are surrounded by total stillness, a great silence, complete peace, a holy quietude. The earth is far away now, the size of a golf ball.

Now you are released from all the petty squabbling, the in-fighting, the hatreds, the jealousies, the nagging guilts. You are free of God-obscuring selfishness.

Your soul is free. You are beyond your troubles, your problems, your anxieties. You breathe freely and cleanly. Yes, you are free, alone in the boundless, soundless, vast area of space.

This is sacred space. It is all-encompassing, all-relaxing. It is beautiful, filled with silence, filled with peace.

You feel engulfed by unlimited love. It is the love of eternal God. This is the home of peace and love.

Affirm to yourself:

I have risen above my tensions.
I am at peace with God.

WHEN YOU FEEL TRAPPED

Do you feel trapped—that you are locked in and blocked—that your problems are fencing you in, making it difficult to move, to do the right thing, to make the right decisions? Try this meditation:

You are trapped in a courtyard which is surrounded by a high iron fence. There is a gate but it is as high as the fence. A chain and padlock keep it securely shut. Walking to the gate you grip the cold iron bars with your bare hands. Every one of your muscles strains as you try to move the gate. All that happens is that the chain rattles and the lock twists around.

Suddenly you hear someone coming from the outside. You see His face. It is a friendly face. It is Jesus Christ. He has keys in His hand and you hear them rattle. He smiles at you as He unlocks the padlock. The chain falls off and the gate swings open.

You run out—across the free, open spaces. Free at last. Now you can affirm:

> I am free at last. Christ has set me free.
> Christ has given me peace.

WHEN YOU FEEL ANGER AND RESENTMENT

Here is a meditation to try when you are riled up, angry, upset, and resentful at your treatment at the hands of someone else. Free yourself of these negative emotions.

Picture yourself in a small boat on the waters of a lake whose surface is being mauled by strong winds. You are rowing the boat toward the shore, and the trip is treacherous. High, rough waves slap strongly against the sides of your helpless little boat. The boat twists one way, then another. Your face feels the sting of the angry water as a wave washes over the prow. You are buffeted on all sides by ferocious wind and water. The wind roars in your ears. The waves hitting your boat sound like cannon shots.

You want to strike back but you can't. It isn't possible. Just ahead you spot a tranquil bay. As your boat rounds the point into the bay, the force of the wind and the water subsides. You are almost clear of the violent elements. As you move slowly into the snug little harbor, calm takes over. There are no waves here. The wind is minimal, finally it is gone. Now you can see the reflections of the trees and surrounding mountains in the cool clear mirrored surface of the lake. The only sound you hear is the soft swish of white water against the nearby beach. Then, you hear the singing of a bird, the chirp of a cricket. All is peaceful now.

With this scene planted in your mind, affirm:

I am calm now. I am free from anger. I am free from resentment. Christ has given me peace.

Like all of us you have probably made your share of mistakes. Perhaps you have sinned and feel guilty. You start to hate yourself. Then you find that you are suffering from the tensions of self-condemnation, regret, and remorse.

Stop. Go into a quiet room or a tree-lined park or an empty church. Any place where you can be quite alone. Close your eyes and visualize: It is winter now in a distant place. Picture a snow-covered hillside crisscrossed by the tracks of skis and toboggans and marred by the footprints of many visitors. The beautiful white snowy slope has become an unsightly scene, much like an old white sheet that has turn tattletale gray, frayed, worn, and torn.

Now it begins to snow. The large, pure, new, white snowflakes start to float gently on the desolate mountainside. At first, a few, then as the snowfall gathers momentum, many more shower down on the hill. They fall silently in a white curtain of soft forgiveness. The snow continues to fall through the afternoon, into the night. Finally, it is morning. The sky is clear now and the golden sun lights up a thick blanket of new snow covering every bit of the hillside. The barren trees are gently draped in soft white feathery velvet. Every mark and ugly blotch on the hill has been covered and is now unseen. The hillside has been forgiven. Now affirm to yourself:

Christ has forgiven me, all my sins are wiped away forever, I am peaceful within.

Now you are able to forgive yourself and your tensions are reduced.

What to Do When You Want to Feel the Presence of Christ

Begin by acquainting yourself with the facts. He is alive. He promises, "I am with you always." God is alive. His presence is blocked from your consciousness by tensions and distractions. Remove the veil that separates His Spirit from your awareness. Begin by blocking out the distractions of the eye, and of the outside world. Close your eyes, now breathe deeply, exhale slowly. Relax. Turn on the natural relaxation response.

When you are fully relaxed, wait until you feel the inner stillness.

Be still and know that I am God. (Psalms 46:10)
Be still before the Lord, and wait patiently for him. (Psalms 37:7)

Meditate on the words of Jesus. Behold, I stand at the door, and knock: *if any man will open the door I WILL COME IN*. (Revelation 3:20)

Now ask God to come into your life. Ask His Holy Spirit to come into your soul. Ask Jesus Christ to come to you.

Now, picture an open field. Picture someone walking across that field. At first you don't recognize Him but you sense that He is a friend. He is a beautiful person, one of your closest friends, but, as yet, you cannot place Him. As He comes closer you can tell by His stride that it *is* Jesus Christ. *It is Jesus Christ, your Savior.*

He lifts His head and sees you. Now you see His face. He calls out to you and runs toward you. His arms open to receive you. He is your Lord. You are neither embarrassed nor ashamed as you open your arms and He embraces you. There in that silent, peaceful field He holds you. He loves you.

Draw Jesus into your life and you'll soon have a peace-centered heart and mind. It will help you face the storms and vicissitudes of life.

Remember the words of the hymn:

What a friend we have in Jesus,
All our sins and griefs to bear.
What a privilege to carry
Everything to Him in prayer.

IX

Beyond Meditation— Two-way Prayer

The peaceful, serene, tranquil, restful feeling that comes through deep meditation is the most wonderful experience in the world. Right? Not quite!

The tension-releasing experience of meditation can be compared to the blessed relief felt after you have crossed a stormy sea, entered a quiet harbor, and rest blissfully, peacefully, at anchor in the bay. That is the end and declared purpose of most meditation today.

PTM offers something more! What can be a better experience than crossing a stormy sea and entering a quiet harbor? It is stepping off the ship, onto the shore, into the warm embrace of your family, sharing the news since last you talked. The relaxation response built into us by our God is there for a purpose beyond the immediate pleasure of peace. God's intention is to relax us so that we *can come across to His side* and talk and fellowship with Him. Remember the theme of this book: "Tranquillity is Conditioning for Creative Communication."

The most exciting spiritual exercise you can ever learn in any book is two-way prayer—the fantastic experience of talking to God, and listening to God in your moments of deep relaxation and PTM. PTM is Possibility Thinking Meditation because in our relaxation response the negative tensions, that would block the flow of creative ideas from God, are removed. The channel is clear. PTM really works! It permits the spiritually healthy mind set which makes it possible for God to send His signals to you. When you are relaxed in meditation, exciting possibility thoughts flow into your mind! After you have meditated to 1. neutralize, 2. harmonize, 3. sterilize, 4. tranquillize and 5. visualize, you can now Possibilitize. Your mind will dream up great ideas, and your imagination will be stimulated with wonderful possibilities!

The purpose of PTM is to achieve a oneness with God in order for Him to be close enough to speak to you! That's what we call two-way prayer. Even as Dr. Herbert Benson suggests that we have a built-in relaxation-response mechanism, Dr. Viktor Frankl, the esteemed psychiatrist, suggests that there may be in human beings a built-in, spiritual mechanism which allows us to pick up God's voice. We recognize this as "the conscience," which Dr. Frankl compares to the navel. "Our navel doesn't make sense unless you recognize men's pre-natal state," the doctor points out. We know, of course, the body was once in a mother's womb, and that the navel was the connection, by way of the umbilical cord, to the mother's body; an arrangement designed to provide nourishment to an embryo incapable of sustaining itself. If we did not have this knowledge the navel simply wouldn't make any sense at all!

Likewise the conscience is a phenomenon that has defied and still defies explanation by psychiatrists. Human beings experience what can only be called "existential guilt capacity." The conscience is a built-in "voice." Studies have proven that it is not necessarily related to pre-conditioning. Only man experiences guilt. The dog who runs when he has misbehaved is not experiencing guilt—he is responding to a conditioned reflex. Pavlovian psychologists have proven this. But humans among all animals experience guilt . . . which is the mind *passing moral judgments on itself*.

The conscience, Dr. Frankl rightly argues, doesn't make any sense (like the navel) unless we recognize man's transcendent nature. When we recognize the Bible's claim that persons are created by God—in His image—and that He created us with a conscience *in order to speak to us, guide us, and direct us,* the conscience makes sense. Then the conscience is God's voice box built in every person. And the conscience, which we normally think is only a negative, judgmental voice box, is in fact the spiritual voice box of God that can be used to allow Him to communicate positive messages. Dreams! Ideas! Sentences! Words! So PTM provides meditation with the positive possibility of making two-way communication a reality between the transcendent Eternal God and His children called human beings! This I believe with all my heart. I have tried it. I live by it. It's exciting—two-way prayer!

Four Levels of Prayer

There are, if I may review for you, four levels of prayer.

The first level, the lowest level of prayer, is Petition. Petitionary prayer is when you call out to God and ask Him for something you need.

It is legitimate prayer, perfectly acceptable in the sight of God. However, it is inclined to be selfish in its basic approach. You are asking for something for *yourself,* even though it is something you need. You do, however, have a need for His help, so it is perfectly fitting and proper to ask for it.

The next level of prayer is called Intercession. At this level prayer is less selfish because you are praying to God for someone else. You are interceding on behalf of some other person—someone perhaps who is ill or in pain or is troubled or grief-stricken. You are praying to the Almighty, asking that He heal them, or ease the pain or take their troubles away.

We then arrive at the third level of prayer which we call Praise. In this kind of prayer you thank God for what He has done on behalf of yourself or others. You pour out your joy, gratitude, and love to Him. You praise Him for his goodness to us all.

We then come to what my friend the late Dr. Frank Laubach called "two-way prayer," the highest form of prayer. In this method of prayer, you engage in intimate conversation with God. You are not necessarily petitioning or interceding or praising. You are communicating with Him and He is communicating with you.

In two-way prayer you are trying urgently and sincerely to seek God's guidance and receive the message He obviously desires to send to you.

In two-way prayer you speak to God and He speaks to you. You hear Him, not with the two visible ears that are on your head with which you hear the voices of people and the sounds of the earth, but with your inner ear. Psychoanalyst Theodore Reik calls this listening with the third ear—your inner ear.

When you hear the voice of God within you, you derive peace and power through prayer. Miracles begin to happen in your life. You become strong in your resolve to achieve the things you have decided to accomplish. God gives you a peace-centered mind from which you

146

derive the power to overcome life's adversities and the strength to find solutions to problems of living.

There are those who do listen with the inner ear deep in their subconscious mind. It is what some psychologists call total integration. The ideas penetrate without emotional blockage.

God speaks to you through your inner ear. When you listen to Him your life is transformed. In two-way prayer you ask Him questions, you wait and hear Him with your inner ear.

How is it possible to hear His voice and receive His spirit?

How do you catch a dove?

At San Juan Capistrano on the southern California coast there are many white doves. When my children were young I would take them there. They would run after the doves, trying to catch them. They were sure they could. They would slowly move up from behind and just as they reached out to capture one, the dove would fly away.

The only way to catch a dove is to put your hand out and wait. Then the dove will come to you and sit in your hand.

The only way to hear God's voice and find His answers is to patiently wait.

There are millions of people who will tell you that they've been praying all their lives and that it really didn't do much for them. But they've probably *never* prayed two-way prayer! They simply called out, "Dear God" or "Our Father" or "Lord," blurted out a steady stream of words, and signed off with an "Amen." Then, raising their heads and standing up, they returned to their work. Never did they *meditate,* relax—wait—and give God a chance to talk to them! They never spent any time listening. Why, they didn't even take the time to hear what God wanted to say to them!

The truth is—these same persons may be equally weak and failing in their other communications with their fellow human beings. You know people who burst into a room, dominate the conversation, do all the talking, don't listen and don't ask for opinions or advice. Having unloaded their inconsiderate and thoughtless baggage of verbiage, they turn on their heel, "Sorry, I've got to go, see you later." The door slams and they've gone. They didn't give you a chance to comment, to question, or respond. That's communication? Hardly!

True communication in all interpersonal relationships does not mean that you do all the talking, dominate the conversation, and leave. You can never build a relationship with anyone unless you spend as much time listening as you do in talking.

In effective two-way prayer you not only talk but you listen. You ask questions and you wait for the answers. You do this with a humble attitude. You assume: "I don't know everything. I've got a lot to learn."

In the book of Jeremiah, we hear the voice of God saying:

Call to me and I will answer you, and will tell you great and hidden things which you have not known. (33:3)

Someone once asked me, "What do you really know about prayer?"

"Not everything," I was forced to admit. "I'm not even certain that I know a great deal about it. But I know enough to realize that we live in two worlds. There is the material, everyday world and there is the

148

spiritual world. There are two realities. There is the one we see with our eyes and feel with our hands and hear with our ears. Then, there is the invisible reality of the spiritual world of God."

I know too that prayer was designed as *God's opportunity to speak to us!* Through this inner voice box! But we abuse the opportunity. Misuse the mechanism. And wonder why it won't work.

I know that two-way prayer works. It is not easy however. It requires tough, hard, discipline to make and take the time to close out the pressures of our busy work-a-day world. It requires time first to prepare for prayer by meditating to relax. You cannot rush into meditation and you cannot rush into two-way prayer! Be prepared to set aside no less than fifteen minutes— thirty minutes is far better. Go slowly through the meditation exercises. Neutralize, harmonize, sterilize, tranquillize your mind. Now visualize God (as a person—or a ray of light), and now, having spent ten to fifteen minutes in meditation move beyond meditation to talk—to listen—to have dialogue with the Eternal.

First a word of warning. Because two-way prayer is highly subjective there is always the danger of "hearing" only what we want to hear. There is also the danger of "hearing" only our subconscious desires, instead of God's true voice. For this reason consider these guidelines as safeguards:

1. Read your Bible before prayer. Read the Ten Commandments. (Exodus 20:2–17) Read the Beatitudes. (Matthew 5:3–12) Be sure that any "message" you get that conflicts with the printed word of God is surely not God's voice! For God will not contradict Himself.

2. Check your "answers" against questions that test

the "Christian integrity" of these "answers." I use these questions to "check my guidance":

a. Is this truly loving?

b. Is this truly unselfish?

c. Is this completely true and honest?

d. Is this truly positive and constructive?

Finally, if you have any reason to doubt the "answers" you get in two-way prayer, and if the guidance goes against your better judgment do this:

a. Consult a deeply committed Christian friend who is experienced in two-way prayer. Ask him to join you in prayer. Share your answer. Together the two of you can go back and ask God again. If both of you agree on the answer—then believe! And move ahead.

My friend, the registered nurse I referred to earlier, is also the wife of a Christian minister and a disciplined practitioner and teacher of two-way prayer. One of her students, a dentist, was still a novice when he called her with a problem. "Perky," he said, "I have a patient with a badly abscessed tooth. I've tried everything and nothing helps. Could you try two-way prayer and find my answer?" Perky's first reaction was negative. "I felt he should find this answer himself," she confided, but added, "since, however, he was a beginner, and very sincere, I agreed to try. So I went into two-way prayer and asked God for wisdom. I listened. I waited. I relaxed. I waited. And the word that came into my mind was 'heat.' I thought, Heat?—that can't be, Lord! For heat could cause the infection to spread! I asked God again. I waited. Again I heard the word heat—almost loudly I heard it!

"I called the dentist and said, 'You won't believe the answer I got. And I must tell you—it's your patient—you do what you feel you must do. But I heard the word heat. Now I know that this could be risky, so please feel free to reject it if, in prayer, you do not get this confirmed.' "

The dentist had it confirmed and applied heat. In a matter of hours the patient's inflammation and infection were reduced. Healing quickly followed.

"Tell me, Perky," the dentist questioned his prayer teacher, "as a registered nurse working for an internist, can you think of any reason why heat should have proven as effective as it has?"

Perky answered, "Not really. We use it for sinus problems when there is a natural drainage."

"Oh," the dentist said, "I forgot to tell you—I had established drainage earlier, but now I can understand how the heat would help the infection drain more quickly in this case."

I know of no spiritual teaching more exciting and more scientific than the law of two-way prayer. God becomes personal. A genuine relationship is established. Suddenly God becomes very real—as real and as alive as any other person who talks to you and listens to you.

You will, with daily practice and devotion, become skillful in this dialogue with God. You will be able to handle any tensions—any problem—any difficulty, and find peace of mind by going into PTM and beyond to two-way prayer.

God listens to you, you listen to Him. You are talking together until you are both in deep spiritual harmony. It's fantastic two-way communication.

Some time back I found myself flat on my back in an ambulance being driven down a mountain road. I had had a serious fall from a ladder. Some bones were broken and I also was bleeding from a ruptured kidney.

Lying there in pain in the jolting ambulance, I began two-way communicating, harmonizing prayer.

"Lord," I asked, "why in the world did I fall?"

I heard Him say, "Schuller, it's your own miserable fault. Why did you use such a rickety ladder."

"That's right, Lord," I answered. "It's my own fault. "Am I going to be all right, Lord?" I asked.

"Yes." The answer was immediate.

And so I spent an hour in the ambulance and thoroughly enjoyed (yes! I honestly did!!) the most wonderful two-way conversation with Him all the way to the emergency room of the hospital.

"You look pretty happy for a guy who's had a bad fall," the doctor in the emergency room declared. If only he knew!

You can use two-way prayer any time you need guidance, comfort, companionship, wisdom, or courage. The basic rule is: Be honest with God! If you have doubts—start there. You might try this two-way prayer:

"God—I've got a problem, don't I?"

(Pause—wait—listen. Chances are you'll hear him say, "Yes, you do.")

"God—right now I even have doubts about you! Where are you? Why don't you say something?"

(Pause—wait—listen. He will answer. He will send a thought, a message, a signal.)

"God—can you help build my faith?"

(Pause—wait—listen. You'll hear him answer? "Yes"—and he may add, "If you will . . ." or, "Yes, but . . .") As I'm writing this book I can testify that God is using two-way prayer to guide me—personally—in the most amazing experience any minister I know of has ever gone through.

In using two-way prayer I suggest and teach that you practice the habit of asking questions that God can answer with a simple "Yes" or "No." Jesus taught this in the Sermon on the Mount: Let your communication be "Yes" and "No." When, therefore, I found people being turned away because our church was too small, I asked God several questions. And He answered me. The dialogue went something like this:

QUESTION: Is it your will that they be turned away?

ANSWER: No.

QUESTION: Do you want me to build a larger church? (I didn't want to! It would mean so much money and I had no resources for such wealth. Furthermore it would create a lot of criticism for me, and I could be sure of that! And I did not welcome the threat of a too large new auditorium that might have empty seats and make me look like a failure!)

ANSWER: Yes.

QUESTION: But, God—where will I get the money?

ANSWER: I will provide.

QUESTION: But, God—it will cost millions—I said millions—of dollars! I don't know any super-rich people!

ANSWER: I do!

And so we moved ahead. Through two-way prayer we hired an architect—and came up with a gorgeous all-glass cathedral. "Ten million dollars!?" I was stunned by the architect's report. Again I went into two-way prayer, "How is it possible?" I asked. "Find ten people to give one million each," I heard. I almost laughed! What I can tell you now is unheard of! On Maundy Thursday I called on a person I had met only briefly. In two-way prayer I was directed to ask him for one million dollars. He answered, "I'd like to, Dr. Schuller, but I can't!" We went into two-way prayer together.

QUESTION: Lord, he'd like to, but he can't. Is it possible for you to find a way for him to do it? Somehow? Sometime? (We paused. We waited. We listened.)

QUESTION: God (I asked aloud) was this Schuller's idea—or yours?

We paused. We waited. We listened. Question followed question. A long silence followed each question. The questions themselves, I feel sure, were unplanned as far as I was concerned. They were very spontaneous. In fact, I was shocked when I heard some of these questions coming from my mouth. After ten minutes I left. The next day, Good Friday, he dialed me to say God had directed him to say "Yes" and he assured me he'd find a way to do it. Within four weeks he delivered the gift! One million dollars! And six weeks later another three persons—for a total of four—had committed for one million dollars each! It appears, in fact, that ten persons will be giving one million each. I can honestly say this would *never*, I repeat *never*, have been our strategy and hence our success if we had not been deeply committed to and practicers of PTM and two-way prayer.

Now face your every decision—your every tension with PTM and two-way prayer and you'll find incredible peace of mind.

X

The Secret of Inner Peace

It was nearly midnight and our ship was passing through the Sea of Marmara, that narrow stretch of water connecting the Dardanelles with the Aegean Sea. My wife and I were on a Mediterranean and Middle Eastern tour, retracing the path of St. Paul, visiting the cities and sites where the great apostle preached.

As we stood on the ship's main deck in the stillness of a moonlit night, we could see the nearby shorelines on both sides of the cruiser. Here and there lights flickered on the black hills silhouetted in the distance against a clear, deep blue sky, lighted by a full moon. The sea was as smooth as glass as the ship slipped silently over the silvery surface. Slowly and softly she moved into the channel the way one reverently enters a great cathedral.

The engine sound had been reduced, now to a low hum, the way loud voices drop to a whisper in a beautiful chapel. The only other sound was the soft swish of the ship's prow slicing through the water—a sound as soft and lovely as a bride's veil brushing over a white satin runner on the way to the altar.

As we stood on the deck, the spirit of absolute serenity reached deeply within us. Not a word was spoken. The silence alone was eloquent enough. Inner Peace! Once you have experienced it you'll never forget it.

The deepest source and sensation of serenity is, however, not to be found in nature but, rather, in the realm of religion. Ultimately, I have to say that what you really need is a vital, deep religion. As he came to the close of his life, Carl Jung, unquestionably one of the greatest psychiatrists of all time, wrote, "During the past thirty years, people from all the civilized countries over Europe have consulted me. I have treated many hundreds of patients. Among all my patients over the age of thirty-five, there was not one whose problem in the final analysis was not that of finding a religious outlook on life. It is safe to say, then, that every one of them fell ill because they lost that which the living religions of every age had given to their followers. And I would say that not one patient in thirty years under my care was ever really healed unless he regained a healthy, religious outlook."

The secret of inner peace is kept in a spiritual treasure chest. From time immemorial, millions of human beings have testified that the most profound peace of mind enfolded them when they encountered an authentic religious experience. I recently received this letter from a prominent southern California psychologist.

Dear Reverend Schuller:

I have "accidentally" tuned in to watch bits and pieces of your ministry on Hour of Power over the past two years. I say accidentally because during most of my life I have been a professed, logical, and closed-minded atheist, which it pains me even to write at this point in my growth. But I was strong in my disbelief. But in spite of my conviction, or lack of it, there was something about you that intrigued me.

In spite of my hard-headedness and negative

156

conceptualization of the state of man, I caught myself actually watching you project deep love that intrigued and fascinated me. You have a way of throwing out sincere peacefulness and great giving over those TV waves. What I am really saying to you is that you brought little glimpses of God's way into my life even when I struggled to resist Him.

Over the course of the past several months I have been working on improving my life to bring joy and happiness to my patients and everyone I encounter. Without realizing it then, I was preparing myself for a wonderful gift. On June 9 of this year my wife and I were sitting in our living room and *I had a religious experience!* I know that I was in the presence of God for a brief moment—yes, me, the all-out nonbeliever. He touched me and it was like *returning home,* returning back to every person, place, experience, and memory in my life that was beautiful and joyful. A sense of going home mixed with grief, nostalgia, elation, release, great understanding, peace of mind, and all I could say over and over again, was "Thank You, Thank You." Thank You for letting me know You before it was too late. Thank You for this infinitesimal glimpse, a single grain of sand on the beach, thank You for this gift of seeing what You have in store for mankind. And I tell you, Bob (if I may take the liberty), that since this wonderful moment my life has changed completely.

All the doubts are gone. The logic and reason and scientific explanations are meaningless. There is no more worry. I finally know what I have been looking for for so very long—peace of mind. And the most wonderful of all: My faith in God is 100%.

I read the Bible many times daily and am so very ignorant and love learning the way. And it surprises even me that I am actively talking about God, love, and the Bible in my sessions with patients, and have even given several Bibles to them. Yes, He does work in mysterious ways.

And I know that my mission here is not to teach or preach or speak in tongues, but to *do it,* to live it, to bring love and the spirit of Christ to everyone I meet every day.

To enjoy the ultimate possibility of inner tranquillity then, seek to venture and acquire a personal religious faith.

If you have followed me from the beginning I trust that you have developed or are developing a positive self-image.

After you have achieved a positive self-image you will be *emotionally capable* of becoming a believer. The non-self-loving person considers himself too unworthy to be loved by God. And you cannot believe in someone who does not love you. "Thou shalt love thy God and thy neighbor—as thyself!" Jesus said you cannot and you will not be able to love God if you despise and hate yourself.

If you hold an unattractive self-image you cannot believe that you were created by a God who is portrayed as "the creator of all things bright and beautiful." The negative decision of such a despairing soul is to doubt or deny God.

To believe in someone is to respond positively toward their first overtures of attention and affection. But surely you will not respond to someone's gestures of love if you feel that a relationship will only expose your unattractiveness, which will result in rejection! So the non-self-loving person cannot bring himself to respond to God's first signals to start a relationship. In the first place, he thinks, God would reject him when God really finds out what an unattractive failure he really is! So his fear of rejection takes the form of simple doubt or denial.

Likewise the non-self-loving person is haunted by guilt. (He has not learned to handle his imperfections.) And guilty persons will go to any length to avoid public trial and judgment. The overweight person avoids the scale, the debtor fears the telephone and mail box, and the guilty sinner avoids religion. So religious doubt or denial becomes the subconscious defense mechanism of a guilty person whose negative self-image will not allow him to believe in a God who might prove to be his judge.

Faith in God—to a non-self-loving person—is the ultimate threat.

Furthermore, religious unbelief is often the projection of one's own lack of faith in himself. Projection is a subconscious defense mechanism where we "judge others by ourselves." The kind person believes others are kind. The dishonest person believes others are dishonest. The person with a negative self-image doesn't believe in himself so how can God believe in him? And how can you believe in someone who doesn't believe in you? His religious doubt is a projection of his self-doubt.

By contrast the person who has an affirmative impression of himself responds naturally, normally, immediately to other positive persons he meets. The secure person intuitively senses secure persons when he encounters them and immediately there is a trusting mental climate that encourages open communication which makes a meaningful relationship possible. So the self-assured person is naturally inclined to respond positively to God when he is introduced to Him.

Faith in God, then, is the natural, normal, positive emotional reaction of a self-respecting person. So, as your positive self-image matures, you will, more and more, become the emotionally healthy person capable of becoming a believer in God. And as your faith grows you will be exposed to the secret of real inner peace.

Tension—A Spiritual Disease

Tension, at its deepest level, is a disease of the spirit. The bird is at ease flying in the air. The fish is at ease swimming in the water. The human spirit is at ease in the religious environment. Faith is man's natural habitat. The proof of it is in the positive results of positive religion: Faith produces these fruits: Peace, Joy, Love, Hope, Courage, Enthusiasm. The proof of it is seen by the contrasting alternative: Doubt produces, in the personality, negative emotions: Fear, Suspicion, Anxiety, Worry, Hostility, Despair.

To eliminate tension at the deepest level seek now a positive faith which heals the human spirit of that disease we call tension.

Now a positive faith in God brings peaceful healing to your mind by offering:

1. Pardon: which removes the tension of guilt.
2. Pride: which eliminates the tension of shame.
3. Purpose: which attacks the tension of meaninglessness. Let's pursue these three steps to serenity:

Pardon is the first and most important step to inner peace of mind and spirit.

Some years ago I was playing chess with Dr. Karl Menninger, the eminent psychiatrist, at the Chicago home of our mutual friend, W. Clement Stone. Out of the blue, Dr. Menninger looked at me and asked, "Dr. Schuller, do you practice repentance?" Since I had been concentrating on the chessboard, I was slightly taken aback by the question. Before I could answer, Dr. Menninger went on, saying, "Nothing will bring healing quicker to people than repentance. They're sinners and they know it. They're responsible for their guilt. They'll never be healthy until they confess and repent before God."

Some people are fearful of confessing their sins before God. They view the Lord as a vengeful, fearful being.

George Bernard Shaw was once asked, "If you were God and could give orders to Noah, who would you select to take on the ark?" The cynical author's response was, "I'd let them all drown."

Martin Luther commented: "If I were God and the world treated me the way it has treated God, I'd have kicked the whole thing to pieces long ago."

I sense that many people in this world secretly believe that God operates in the spirit expressed by Shaw and Luther. No wonder they hesitate to rush penitently to Him.

The word gospel means good news. The gospel of Jesus Christ is the good news that God is not in the mold of Luther and Shaw, but is more like the reflection seen in the words and deeds of Jesus Christ.

Christ demonstrated such non-judgmental love that people flocked to Him, found and accepted forgiveness for their sins. He saw the potential for good in even the worst of people. He wanted to bring out the best in them. How? By helping them to be redeemed from the guilt that kept reinforcing their negative self-image.

God's forgiveness is total and complete. Ask Him for salvation and the very memory of your sins will be wiped out. "As far as the East is from the West, so far has He removed our transgressions from us."

St. Paul shared the secret of serenity in these words: "Therefore being justified by faith we have peace with God through our Lord Jesus Christ." Christians believe that if we have faith—that is—come to God and trust that He will forgive us—that He indeed will forgive us! Then we will experience the peace of being "justified" for God will treat us:

"Just-as-if-I'd" never sinned.

"Just-as-if-I'd" never done anything wrong.

"Just-as-if-I'd" never felt guilty.

When this happens, you have made your peace with God! You will feel the mantle of spiritual calm descending upon you that bestows a peace that is indescribable.

The lovely twenty-six-year-old girl was trembling as she sat before me, in my counseling office. She struggled to regain her composure in order to tell me her problem.

"I'm married," she said. "I have a three-year-old son. Some months ago I discovered that I was pregnant once again. I wasn't too happy. My mother said, 'Get rid of it.' My husband said, 'Get rid of it.' So, I did. Right there," and she pointed in the direction of the county hospital, a half-mile away.

She continued with her story, but now her whole body was shaking and tears poured from her eyes, as she was convulsed by feelings of guilt and shame. "I feel sure I killed a beautiful, budding life and it's driving me crazy. It might have been a beautiful little girl."

I stood up and taking her by the hand, I led her to my Savior. I shared with her the words of Jesus spoken from the Cross. "Forgive them, Father, for they know not what they do."

Then, I told her, "He can save you. He can forgive you. His cross proves that He can and will forgive any sin." She then accepted Jesus Christ as her personal Savior. The expression on her face was miraculously transformed from one of turmoil and torture to one of tranquillity. Her body was relaxed now.

Do this now. Pray this prayer. "O God, I, too, need forgiveness. In Your saving love, forgive and cleanse me. Jesus Christ, I believe You are the forgiving God. I affirm You have saved me. You love me. I am justified by faith. I have peace with God through Jesus Christ. Amen."

You are now ready to experience Christian Pride. PRIDE. (Enjoy a rebirth of self-worth.)

When guilt goes, shame goes. Once you are pardoned, a sense of pride will return. You no longer will suffer from self-rejection. You will experience self-acceptance. When God forgives you, He takes you in with Him. You become a somebody now.

The Christian who is "saved" or "born again" or "converted" is proud to walk with Christ. We look up to Him with admiration and affection. Through our subconscious mind we seek to emulate Him in our daily lives. Identifying closely with Him, we develop a new self-image.

There is the legend of a man who allowed himself to become round-shouldered through a lifetime of poor posture. So he asked a sculptor to cast a statue of him in a perfectly straight, upright position, shoulders back, head held high, chin up—just the way he looked when he was in the prime of life.

When the man received his statue, he hid it in a remote corner of his wooded garden. For a few minutes every day he would go to the hiding place and contemplate himself as he once was. Without realizing it he would straighten up as he gazed on the statue.

As time went on the man's friends noticed that he was standing straighter, regaining his youthful posture. One day his granddaughter, seeing him walking through the garden, decided to follow him. At the secret hiding place she was startled to see what appeared to be two grandpas.

One was shining like a golden god in the sun, straight and tall, the other standing nearby was a more stooped version of the first. Then, as she watched, the real grandfather stood straighter and straighter. The granddaughter cried out, "Grandpa, you're standing straight, too, just like the other grandpa."

He had become like the image of himself which he had created.

If you hold in your mind the image of yourself as you would like to be, of the person God wants you to be, you can become that person. Think of yourself as tall and strong, in a spiritual sense, and you will have an image to emulate.

You will love yourself as never before. And self-love rooted in a relationship with God becomes the all-important step in casting out the tensions in your life in order to build a peace-centered quiet mind which will develop the power needed for an abundant, fulfilled, happy life.

Here is a prayer to help you attain this state.

Christ, I know you want to live your life in me. I want to be like you. I want to love people the way you would love people. I open my eyes to see you, to become like you, I open my heart to allow you to love people through me. I love myself now as I feel your love flowing through me. Amen.

You are ready now to be healed from the tension of meaninglessness.

PURPOSE—(PUT A SOUL IN YOUR GOAL)

What is your purpose in living? Do you have a soul in your goal?

Now as a redeemed, forgiven human being with a healthy ego, touched by Christ, you will be inspired to be a healthy, helpful somebody. Insecure people indulge in vanity to feed their uncertain and shaky egos.

An ancient Chinese parable tells of an emperor who was so insecure, so lacking in self-confidence, so tension-torn, that he kept himself sheltered in his palace. In an attempt to bolster his confidence he would gaze at his reflection in a large mirror. In this way he would assure himself that he was a great ruler. His sole goal in life seemed to be to impress himself with his own importance. While he remained interested only in himself, his people were being hoodwinked by officials who confiscated their lands. Reduced to a state of extreme poverty, they were hungry and worn. Misery abounded in the streets.

A wise member of the palace staff, realizing the need for the emperor to take action, devised a plan. One night the courtier removed the mirror. In its place he cut a window in the wall, the same size and shape as the mirror. When the emperor arose he proceeded, as was his custom, to stand before the mirror. This time, however, instead of his own reflection, he saw his subjects in the street below, huddled together in their misery. He saw weary women carrying burdens on their backs. He saw hungry children scurrying around looking for scraps of good. He saw tired old men and young men in rags.

The emperor cried out, "What happened to my poor people?"

The loyal friend who had engineered the plan told him what had been happening. Losing all care for himself, the emperor went out among his people. From that time on, he took a personal interest in his subjects. Prosperity returned to the land and the people were content and hungry no longer.

Christ does this to you—and to me. He transforms the mirror in your life to a window on the world. He causes us to forget about ourselves and become interested in people and their problems. Then He gives us the self-confidence we need to go out and help those who are hurting. He gives us a purpose in living; He puts a soul in our goal.

Robert Louis Stevenson, the author of *Treasure Island* and many other famous books, always remembered one of his earliest childhood memories. He would watch from his bedroom window as the old lamplighter came down the street in Edinburgh, Scotland, as darkness fell, lighting the oil lamps, one by one. Many years later, Stevenson recalled, "What I remember best about that lamplighter; he always left a light behind him."

Are you leaving lights behind you? Are you inspiring others to greatness?

What is the most beautiful sight on earth? Confucius, China's greatest philosopher, said, "The most beautiful sight in the world is a little child going confidently down the road after you have shown him the way."

You can and will be that kind of a person if Christ's Spirit motivates you! You will discover a new reason for living! And Christ needs you, for there are so many lost souls who need to rediscover life's basic values. You can help. The greatest joy in the world can come from pointing lost persons in the right direction.

When people ask me where I found meaning in life, I point to Christ and say, "He gave me pardon, He gave me pride; He has given me a purpose in living."

Do you have an awareness of God's presence in your life? I do. And it heals me from tension and gives me deep serenity and peace. I know that a divine destiny is guiding my path as I move from hour to hour, from day to day, into the unknown future. I have a confident sense that Someone is leading the way and shaping my future.

This will be true for you, as well, if you will sincerely pray this Serenity Prayer.

Christ, beautiful Savior,
Grant me Pardon.
Restore my Pride
Inspire me purposely so to live in your Spirit,
that I may point
lost persons down the right road
and in my walk may I
leave lights behind me
wherever I go.
I know
your presence will never leave
me in my future walk
with you. Amen.

Follow this threefold path and you'll find a new life, with a confident feeling of serenity and peace of mind growing within you.

Does this mean that you will never have any more

167

trouble or upsetting experiences? Does your new faith in God suggest that He will protect you from all hardship and pain? Not so. Rest now in this peaceful assuredness:

"Be confident of this one thing that God who has begun a good thing in you will complete it." (Philippians 1:6)

In the next chapter we will learn how to develop a tough faith for rough times that can enable you to practice poise through Possibility Thinking where you face impossible situations. For if God has (1) pardoned you, (2) bestowed pride into your soul and (3) given you a beautiful purpose in living, surely (4) He will providentially care for you so nothing will happen unless it can be turned into a positive possibility!

XI

Practice Poise Through Possibility Thinking

You can move ahead now, and develop a relationship with God that will give you a tough faith for rough times.

You will have experiences that will prove to you beyond a shadow of a doubt that there is a "great invisible hand" that reaches out to guide you in difficult times, enabling you to face potentially panic-generating situations with amazing calm. Deep down in your heart you know He will work things out right: "And we know that all things work together for good to those who love God and keep His Commandments." (Romans 8:28)

Mary Verghese dreamed her young-girl dreams of becoming an obstetrician. Now she had completed, at long last, her studies and was graduated from Vellore Medical College in her native country of India. She made it! With eleven other celebrating young doctor graduates she jumped into a station wagon to go on a picnic. Then an accident happened. Passing a bus, the driver of the wagon lost control and it rolled over three times. Mary regained consciousness five days later paralyzed from the waist down. "Oh God, I'll never feel warm, squirming babies in my hands," she wept as she saw her dreams snatched forever away. Then, like a miracle of God's mercy, from her memories there came the words of an old hymn. She uttered the words, "Take my hands and let them be Consecrated, Lord, to Thee." Into her room stepped one of India's leading surgeons, Dr. Paul Brandt. "Mary, I think you could be my assistant in surgery. We could build a ramp and you could operate from your chair," he said.

That was many years ago. Today, Dr. Mary Verghese has become one of the most skillful, expert surgeons in transplanting tendons in deformed lepers' hands. Her two hands have become the ten fingers of God. Thousands are happier because of her.

As she says it:

"I asked God for legs‡ and He gave me wings."

"But if there is an all powerful, all loving God, why doesn't He prevent all sickness, sin, and suffering?" That anguished question has been asked by every generation. The answer is clear. God is dealing with *people* who are *persons*—not puppets—and persons have free will. The freedom to choose is what makes us moral creatures. Suppose through genetic engineering, or through Skinnerian Conditioning we could produce people who are sinless and perfect, would that be wonderful? Hardly. We would then have evolved a new species. The result would not be human beings. A human being is a person—not a puppet or a perfect computer. Being a person means that we have the freedom to sin and the freedom to fail. It is in fact that negative possibility that gives value to the positive possibility. Integrity is only affirmed in dialectic. Which means: "Yes" is meaningless if I do not have the freedom to say "No."

Faith is meaningless and empty if it does not come

‡ Dorothy Clarke Wilson, *Take My Hands*, New York: McGraw-Hill, 1963.

from a heart and mind that has the freedom to choose not to believe! So responsible religion does not attempt to indoctrinate. For this wouldn't produce great believers—only polished puppets. Their brainwashed mouthings of "faith-statements" would mean nothing to God. Great religion doesn't indoctrinate—it educates! It is therefore impossible (and I don't use that word lightly) to create a truly totally loving person unless he has the capability and freedom to choose to be nonloving. So when God created *Homo sapiens* He had the *freedom to choose*. Should He create a perfect creature incapable of sin? This would mean that such a creature would be incapable of deciding which would mean incapable of loving. For loving is deciding and loving is choosing. So God decided to create a creature "in His own image" which means persons who have the "freedom to choose to love or not to love": to obey or not to obey Spiritual loves: to believe or not to believe in God!

We all know the result. Original Man (Adam) rebelled (chose to do his own thing to prove to himself he was a great person in his own right) and the whole human predicament was launched. And how could God redeem the situation without destroying the human race? To redesign, re-engineer, and remodel people incapable of imperfection would be to create beautiful robots.

"Yes, God, I love you." "Yes, God, I will obey you." "Yes, God, I love you." The perfect recording would never make a mistake. The "love," however, would be so meaningless it would really not be love. He would have replaced (destroyed) a species—not saved it. So God chose to redeem, not ruin.

God's only alternative was to move into the situation and allow persons the freedom to fail, to make mis-

171

takes, to commit sins, and to practice unbelief. God could then make His redeeming love available to help them turn their troubled lives around. He would give us enough freedom to remain persons but maintain enough control never to allow us to get into such impossible situations that could not and would not contain redeeming possibilities!

Here then is the basis for a mature faith that will enable you to maintain peace in the face of a potential panic! Here, then, is how you use Possibility Thinking to practice poise in threatening times. The greatest authorities in the field of religion unanimously testify to the wonderful way God takes over in our trouble and creates the possibility for us to reap dividends from our difficulties. A great Old Testament believer said "In my distress, Lord, thou hast enlarged me." (Psalm 4:1) A modern paraphrasing could be: "There is no gain without pain." Look for positive possibilities in these dark times and peace of mind will overflow you!

I know from personal experience what panic feels like—and how to change that "panicky" feeling to a powerful, poised feeling.

I was fresh out of Seminary. I graduated one week, took my licensure tests seven days later, and a week after that I was married and headed off to my first church in a Chicago suburb. I had no idea what I was getting into. Here was a tiny congregation of about forty members, split down the middle with suspicion and distrust. Both factions tried to use me for their purposes. To an inexperienced young man this was a most difficult problem. On top of that the church had money problems. And they wouldn't let me talk about money. I found out that the most sensitive nerve in the human body is the one that leads to the pocketbook. Someone said, "Money talks, but it also stops a lot of talk."

172

One night I tossed sleeplessly, worrying about the church. Night after night I had trouble sleeping. Then I dreaded the oncoming night for fear of sleeplessness. Next, I imagined I would suffer from a breakdown if I didn't get more sleep. Guess what? Just at that crucial moment a prominent magazine came out with this headline on the cover: "Why Ministers Are Cracking Up." That night I experienced panic—sudden sweating—the tinge of hysteria. "This is it, Schuller—you're going to flip now. You are about to have a nervous breakdown." I prayed desperately! Into my mind God sent this Bible verse, "All things work together for good to those who love God."

The next thought was also a positive thought: "Perhaps God is trying to teach me something through this experience. If God wants to give me advanced training in understanding human problems by leading me into a firsthand experience with a breakdown—well, in that case a crack-up will be a build-up! So don't fight it or fear it: if it comes, enjoy it," the inner voice said. From that moment on I imagined only great positive possibilities in all potentially trying experiences—and poise replaced panic. I have since identified this feeling of inner poise as the very power and presence of God within me.

Believe that God will let nothing happen to you unless something good will come out of your so-called trouble. How do you develop such a faith? Well, begin by practicing positive thinking, and move on to Possibility Thinking.

In trouble God liberates us. In the wise, loving providence of God, life's difficulties are often liberating experiences. She thought the world was caving in when her husband died—until she practiced Possibility Thinking. Then she announced to me, "I have been liberated. Of course I loved him. But now I'm free to pursue my interests. He was my only project, you know. Now I'll take voice lessons again, and resume my study of the cello." *The eagle stirreth up her nest, that the young might learn to fly.* "Look for possibilities in your problems!" *In my distress thou, Lord, hast enlarged me.*

When the darkness falls the stars come out. God never allows us to suffer without compensations. In one of Ian MacLean's stories, it is a blind girl speaking, "I dinna see but there's nobody in the Glen can hear like me. There's no footstep comes to my door, but my ear tells me his name. The birds sing sweeter to me than to anybody else, and I can hear them cheeping in the bushes before they go to sleep. And the flowers smell sweeter to me—the roses and the carnations and the bonny moss rose. Na, na, you're not to think that I've been ill treated by God, for if there's one thing He didn't give me, many's the lovely things He did give me."

In trouble God educates us. In his book *How to Live a Richer and Fuller Life* (New York: Prentice-Hall, 1951), Rabbi Edgar F. Magnin once wrote, "I recently called on a brilliant and successful young business woman who had undergone an operation that precluded the use of her eyes. I had felt that she would be an uncomfortable patient for she was normally vital and unaccustomed to idleness. The nurse asked me to wait a few minutes before going into her room. 'She has a caller,' the nurse said with an odd smile and what seemed a peculiar emphasis. No one left the room however when the nurse opened the door and announced me. 'You need not have waited,' the patient said in a vibrant and welcoming voice that contrasted with her bandaged eyes, 'it's simply that I won't permit telephone calls to disturb my visitors. Walter Winchell was just here.' 'Walter Winchell? I didn't see him. Does he know you?' I asked. She pointed, laughing, to her radio. 'This morning two senators were here debating foreign policy for me. Later two scholars discussed the writings of Proust. Then I had a complete performance of the New York Philharmonic. Really, Rabbi, it's been a wonderful day! Friends have brought flowers—don't they smell beautiful? And now you've come. I'm beginning to think operations are wonderful!' "

"In my distress, Lord, Thou hast enlarged me."

In trouble, God illuminates us. God will let nothing happen unless He can turn it into an advantage. Use possibility thinking to imagine that God may use your trouble to illuminate your path—or your mind. Viktor Frankl learned powerful psychiatric insights which he later incorporated in Logotherapy. He learned these lessons through his experience in the concentration camps. John Bunyan wrote *Pilgrim's Progress* in prison. The church where I work would not have been developed if it had not been for Rosie Gray—a paralyzed woman who could only come to church in her car. As a result she forced us to plan to build the "Walk-in, Drive-in church," which now ministers to eight thousand people every week.

Too many people will never slow down to hear God's voice until they enter the valley of suffering. If suffering turns you to God, does it not become a blessing? "In the year that King Uzziah died I saw the Lord," Isaiah wrote. Many a father and mother have been converted at the death of a child. "But what good is it to the child?" the cynic asks. I'll let Jesus Christ answer that, "Except a grain of wheat fall into the ground and die it bears no fruit." "He who lives and believes in me shall never die." There is no birth without birth pangs. There is no entrance into eternal life except through the birth experience the world calls death.

175

Facing trial or trouble? Then God is getting ready to illuminate your path or condition you for a life of more effective service. "In love's service only broken hearts will do."

An old Roman said when the Christian system was introduced: "This system cannot stand because it is founded upon a cross, upon the death of its own leader, upon a catastrophe; it cannot stand." And yet we know that that is just why it does stand.

In trouble, God motivates us. A flower has been discovered in South America which is only visible when the wind blows; it is of the cactus species, and when the wind blows, a number of beautiful flowers protrude from the little lumps on the stalks. Trials bring out our deepest love.

As I have mentioned one of the greatest men of this century was the late Reverend Dr. Daniel A. Poling, predecessor of Dr. Norman Vincent Peale as pastor of Marble Collegiate Church in New York. One of my joys is the memory of Dr. Dan's friendship.

He told the story of how God used a crushing experience to motivate him to dedicate his life to greatness in love.

"I was a young man just separated a few months from the Armed Forces where, in France, I prayed over many a dying American. Now I was vacationing in Oregon when I got a call to come home. My young brother was gravely ill. When I saw him in mortal pain with typhoid fever I knew what to do—that night in a room separated from my brother's by a partition so thin I could hear his sharp staccato breathing, I knelt to ask God to keep His promise that had never failed. With complete assurance I began my prayer. But for some reason my prayers got nowhere. They gave me no promise—no peace. I seemed standing in front of a gate of brass that would not open. I argued. I demanded. Gradually a hopelessness came over me—then disillusion—then anger, and finally despair, for I wanted my brother to live more than I desired anything in the world! How I loved him. Some years before, when he first learned to print, he climbed on my lap one night as I was studying. He didn't disturb me; as I read on he labored to print in large block letters his name over his picture—RUDOLPH. Then he slid off my lap—and left his autographed picture on my desk.

"Now he was breathing so hard. More than anything else in the world I wanted him to live. I would gladly have pledged my own life to God in exchange for his. I prayed—but hadn't the slightest indication I was heard. I left the house and tramped beside the little river across the bridge and into the country. I was alone now as never before. Tired to the bone, I came back to my room and back to my knees. Now the breathing beyond the partition had changed. It galloped like a runaway horse! I could not pray any more. Wearily I fell asleep. Hours passed. The dawn came. I opened my eyes. I listened—no breathing. I knew that God had answered my prayer and His answer was 'no.'

"Now the real miracle happened. I was satisfied that God had not made a mistake! Amazing peace came over me. There was no rebellion in me—no bitterness—but a power I had never known before and knew would never leave me. 'O God, let me make something great out of my life. Don't let me waste it,' I prayed. So I know that Rudolph's passing brought peace with power. I am a better man today.

"In my distress, Lord, thou hast enlarged me."

No one understands this "Possibility Thinking in the face of difficulty" better than Jesus Christ.

"If I be lifted up I will draw all men unto me," He

said. By this He referred to His death which was to come on the cross. When He faced His last day He did so with quiet poise. Before Pilate and Herod, and all during His hours of public humiliation, He remained calm. "Have you nothing to say?" Pilate asked. Christ knew that the cross was His greatest opportunity to demonstrate to the human race God's immeasurable forgiving love. "Father, forgive them . . ." He cried.

That happened on Good Friday.

Then came Easter!

Let go, let God take over. Now then—let your worries and fears go—and let God take over your life. Your future will be filled with hope. Are you lacking in hope today? Then surrender your life to God.

"There are no hopeless situations—only hopeless people, only people who think hopelessly," Albert Cliffe wrote.

Among the many letters I receive, is this thrilling true story.

Two weeks before Christmas I was so depressed that I tried to take my life. When I failed, my doctor and my husband made me see a psychiatrist but he couldn't help me by hypnosis or talking to me. I was afraid of the shock treatments which he recommended. Then on Sunday in January, a friend called me and made me promise to do her a favor which was to turn on the TV and listen to your program. I did so, and it was wonderful! It seemed as if you were a lifelong friend talking to me and giving me the helpful advice I needed so dearly. I determined I was going to put myself in the Lord's hands and live each day to its fullest with His help and yours.

That is just what I did and in one week I was

beginning to enjoy life again. In those weeks I was so much improved that I told the doctor I wouldn't need the shock treatments, and now I am happier than I have been in years, and I am confident that I won't ever be mentally sick again.

Never lose hope. Never give up. Never surrender your faith.

FAITH—THE SPARK IN THE DARK

The second oldest college in America is William and Mary, in Williamsburg, Virginia. It is today one of our most prestigious institutions of higher learning.

However, in 1881 the far-reaching effects of the Civil War had created a financial catastrophe—and in this depression, William and Mary closed its doors. It would have remained closed if it had not been for the undying faith of its President, Dr. Benjamin Ewell. Every morning he would rise, walk across the campus to ring the old college bell. It was all he could do—but it said, "I believe in tomorrow. I believe in tomorrow." And one day, the doors opened again!

One of my friends who has experienced how God gives special blessings in troubled times has this sign on his desk, "Hallelujah Anyway!"

Trust God for His loving Providence.

Practice poise and experience peace of mind through Possibility Thinking.

XII

Now Succeed with Peace of Mind

Now you can succeed—in living with peace of mind through Possibility Thinking—if you really want to!

Standing naked before the Gestapo, Viktor Frankl found this great possibility thought pass through his mind: "There is one thing you cannot take from me— my freedom to choose how I will react to what you do to me."

No matter where you are emotionally—this very moment—you have, and will have to your dying breath the freedom to choose.

Choose to secure for yourself peace of mind and you choose to live serenely and successfully.

Power to Succeed Will Now Flow From Your Peace-Centered Mind

The place? Paris, France. The event? The International Congress of Psychologists. The scene? A symposium on Behavioral Modification. The chairman is speaking. "As psychologists, we know a great deal about persons but still we fail to change people. Look around you! The people you know—and chances are that includes you and me—eat too much, or smoke too much, or drink too much, or move around and exercise too little."

What's the answer? The answer is to know the right question. And the right question is: Why do persons deliberately, knowingly, willfully choose to fail? The answer in part at least lies in the deep-seated lack of belief in ourselves to succeed. By nature, all persons are born with a profound assumption that they will fail.

The modern findings of Erik Erikson, pre-eminent specialist in child development, casts the mantle of psychological affirmation on an ancient theological affirmation. In Judaic-Christian theology, it was held that man was "conceived and born in sin." What is the core of the core sin? It is the lack of trust which provokes an insecurity in relationships—an insecurity which results first in defense, then in hostile behavior; and finally in either aggressive conflict or the depressing emotional withdrawal of defeat. When some theologians have been saying that the core of sin is rebellion, they have concluded this penetrating research too quickly. The deeper question is why would people rebel against a beautiful God? The answer lies in man's inherent distrust—he fears failure in his relationships. So rebellion, that tense reaction of an insecure person, is a defensive mechanism set up to protect us from a possible relationship we view, mistakenly, to be a threatening option! So tension disrupts communication! And a vicious cycle is set in motion.

Now Erik Erikson has demonstrated that the newborn infant is born lacking in trust. The first two stages of development, according to Erikson, are, first, from birth to twelve months. This is the stage where a child hopefully learns trust. Birth has been a traumatic experience. Through soft stroking, bathing, breast-feeding if possible, the gentleness of the bath, and soft sounds, the new occupant of our noisy alien culture learns to trust.

The scene is set for stage two: from twelve months to

twenty-four months, the child learns self-confidence. From crawling and creeping, he rises to stand at the chair. Now he feels the thrill of the vertical dimension! He feels tall. He is now challenged to experience (1) individuality; (2) choice; (3) decision; (4) rewards of achievement—"Come to Daddy—you can walk! Come on!" is usually every person's introduction to selfhood. So he tries—and fails; tries again, partially succeeds and partially fails; tries again and finally learns! He has now moved emotionally from trust to some self-confidence. And this is something that must be caught—it cannot be taught.

Tragically—for too many persons the infantile self-belief that has now begun to evolve fails to continue to develop into full blossom. The deep-seated, intrinsic, generic core of self-distrust continues to threaten to assert itself through life, warning the growing person, "Be careful. You may get hurt." Self-confidence, which needs constant nourishment and support to keep growing through childhood, adolescence, and adulthood, can too easily be stunted, throttled, even set back by non-adventurous mental attitudes and experience. So a fear of failure becomes too easily a mind-set that concretizes itself to firmly fix—as in a cement statue—a life pattern. So a fear of failure—rising from a lack of self-trust—becomes a desire to fail: "If I don't try—I'll not fail. So I'll succeed! So the way to succeed is to fail to even try!"

It is this emotional disorder that we call a negative self-image. And this negative self-image is singularly the major emotional disorder that universally entangles human beings in a web of failure-producing mental attitudes. So we fail because we choose to fail. We choose to fail because we don't want to fail. How's that for disorder? But true! Perhaps of you, too!

Who has the cure that can eradicate the deep inner distrust that plagues us with dark prophecies and gloomy predictions of failure?

Your Positive Religious Faith Will Now Boost and Build Life-Changing Self-Confidence

I will long remember the night I was invited to join the luminaries of Hollywood to salute Ethel Waters. It was a great night, but the greatest part of the whole evening was when Ethel Waters herself—in her own inimitable, open, honest, transparent, crystal-clear personality simply told people about how happy she was because Jesus was in her heart! I watched Ethel Waters perform that night and I saw her on the screen as they presented playbacks of her great life. We listened to her sing, and listened to her preach as only Ethel Waters can sing and preach. I thought to myself, if every psychiatrist, psychologist, and philosopher around the world would submit the names of persons who, in their judgment, were the healthiest people emotionally, I will tell you who would win—hands down—Ethel Waters. She knows how to laugh, and she knows how to cry. She is a big heart, she is a great soul, she is alive!

What makes her so alive? The psychologist would guess, "Well, she had a fortunate childhood," until he checks it out and discovers that she was fathered by a rapist. Thank God they did not have easily available abortions in those days or her mother would have aborted her as soon as she found out that the rape resulted in pregnancy. When you discover that she was an illegitimate child, raised in a ghetto, and in poverty— her life puts a lie to some of the great books and treatises that have been written by psychiatrists and psychologists in the past fifty years. By every standard she should have been an emotionally deprived and mentally scarred person, with a severely limited range of potential emotional development.

Analyze Ethel Waters and what do you find? You find the greatest soul that you will find walking the planet earth. How do you explain it? There is no answer except that something gave her a great big, loving, bubbling, beautiful heart. She says that something is a *somebody*—His name is Jesus!

Because she was raised an illegitimate child, knocked around the alleys of the ghetto of her town, and through life, she sang "Stormy Weather" with such feeling! Somebody asked her to sing it that night, and she said, "No, sir, I'm never going to sing 'Stormy Weather' again as long as I live. I can't! I can't! I don't have stormy weather any more. I have peace in my heart because Jesus lives in me."

Man was designed by God as an organism wherein God Himself could live. You will not have emotional health and wholeness until you know God. There is no emotional problem that Christ cannot heal. When God touches your life—He lets you know who you are! And He saves you from self-condemnation to self-confidence when you come to know that you're God's idea and God only has beautiful ideas. In Ethel Waters' immortal words, "God don't sponsor no flops!"

You Will Now Begin to Consider Your Possibilities

As you relax in your relationship with your Eternal God, He will be able to communicate with you in the quiet center at the core of your being. He will unfold amazing possibilities within your "born-again imagination." New and exciting ideas will come to you! Now you will begin to believe in these ideas and you will believe in your own possibilities!

Don't Confuse the Person You Are with the Person You Were or the Person You Will Become

You were an insecure person trying to run your life without God's guidance, direction, wisdom, power, and presence. And in that state, you were naturally anxiety-prone and understandably lacking in self-confidence. If recurring self-doubts return to draw you back or hold you back—do not be confused! You are remembering the person you were!

Today you are a different person. You are God's special idea! And the world has yet to see what great things you can do and what a beautiful person you will become!

Your Self-Confidence Will Grow Ever Stronger as Your Faith Grows into Trust

An enormously powerful self-confidence will rise within you as you turn your life over to God and trust Him. He will give you a great, new, positive self-image. Positive ideas will naturally flow through your mind. And the greatest force in the world is a positive idea in the self-confident mind of a bold believer who is walking with God and trusting his Lord.

I heard this story when I was a little boy going to the country church in Iowa and it has inspired me through the years. "Trust in the Lord and do good," was the minister's text that day. He said, "It's not enough to believe. You have to trust. And there is a difference. And until you learn to trust, you'll never achieve what God wants you to achieve."

Then he told this story: "A stuntman pulled a tight-rope across the waterfalls of Niagara and announced that he was going to walk across both ways. A crowd gathered for the event. He started walking and made it to the other side and the crowd applauded. Then he attempted to walk back; he made it again and everybody applauded. People who said it couldn't be done suddenly became believers. Then he took a wheelbarrow and walked the wheelbarrow across. By this time everyone was a believer where some had been scoffers before. Then he asked, 'Now before I take the wheelbarrow back once more, I'm going to ask for a volunteer. Who will ride in the wheelbarrow?' Applauding believers suddenly drew back! But one young child came forward, and climbed into the wheelbarrow. She demonstrated TRUST. 'Of course,' someone observed correctly, 'the little girl trusts him because he is her father!'"

Trust God. Believe in yourself. Dare to dream! And trust Him enough to put your whole future in His hands.

You've heard it said, "I've got to see it to believe it!" Now you know the truth. The truth is, "I've got to believe it before I see it!" Congratulations, New Believer!

You Will Keep Your New Faith Going, Growing, and Glowing

Now guard and care for this beautiful, peace-producing relationship with God. It is sensitive. It is tender. Treat it carefully and gently or it is forced to live in an emotionally hostile and unfriendly environment.

Carlos B. Romulo, upon returning to the Philippines after spending many years in the United States, left this provocative message: "I am going home, America. Farewell. For seventeen years I have enjoyed your hospitality, visited every one of your fifty states. I can say I know you well. I admire and love America. It is my second home. What I have to say now, in parting, is both a tribute and a warning. Never forget, America, that yours is a spiritual country. Yes, I know you are a practical people. Like others, I have marveled at your factories, your skyscrapers, and your arsenals; but underlying everything else is the fact that America began as a God-loving, God-fearing, God-worshiping people. And so again I say in parting, Thank you, America, and farewell. May God keep you always and may you always keep God."

The question is, "How do we keep God in the quiet center of our lives?" God Himself gave that to His Chosen People when He gave the Law and the Ten Commandments to Moses—God's way to the Good Life: God's Prescription for Peace of Mind. Live by their deep and profound spirited principles to keep your faith growing.

You Will Establish Your Faith-Building, Peace-Producing Quiet Zone

"Remember the Sabbath day to keep it holy" is one of those great Ten Commandments you will use to keep your faith growing. Perhaps no single discipline is more relevant to American culture today than this word from the Lord. We cannot expect God to speak to us until we are quiet, calm, and relaxed. Tranquillity is Conditioning for Communication! We cannot all live in the Garden of Eden. We must deal with buses, trucks, concrete, and asphalt. The answer is in designing both in space and in time, structured quiet zones. In time—

you will design and structure one day a week to be a supremely treasured and protected twenty-four-hour period of time when the mind and heart and soul can be withdrawn from the day-after-day bombardment of tension-producing sights, sounds and smells. Remember the Neutra Principle Realism. God must communicate to a spirit that dwells in a Biological Organism.

This weekly quiet zone in time should be a period of time beginning at sundown and continuing for twenty-four hours, as practiced by many Jews. In our family, as traditional Christians, we start our sabbath observance with the Saturday night meal. Almost never in our first twenty-five years of marriage would we ever permit ourselves as parents, or our children as children, or our family as a unit, to go out on Saturday nights. A quiet meal. A quiet home. A quiet night. Family prayers after the Saturday night dinner. Relaxing baths. The mind goes to bed on this one night of the week beginning to relax, prepared to experience a spending of this relaxation through the spirit during a night of calm sleep.

In the morning the mind is conditioned for the most unique day of the week. This day is for worship and the family—for rest and peace and gladness.

The clothing we put on is distinctive. It will be clothing that will harmonize with the highest emotions of self-esteem and self-dignity.

The place to which we go is distinctive—the house of worship. The people we gather together with are distinctive—they are seekers after peace—love—faith—hope. The sounds, sights, smells are distinctive—rhythms of light, fragrances of flowers, tempo and harmonies and intensity of sounds are distinctive—to contribute to peace and joy and gladness! The words we hear are distinctive. Tension-producing profanity which we must tolerate in public, in print and through other media through the week is replaced by "different words." And words are emotional bullets or emotional baths—Sunday is an exposure to words that cleanse, relax, and heal the spirit!

We leave this experience of worship having had a two-sided therapeutic treatment. We have—in worship—drained out the negative emotions and tensions—that inevitably collect every six days. And we have filled our lives at a deep level with a Positive Emotional Experience. As the oil of an engine is drained out to carry with it the collected invisible irritants that would silently but cancerously corrode the power center of the engine, so we have given ourselves a "spiritual oil change."

Now we return from the house of worship to an environment which is emotionally harmonious with the scene set the night before and enhanced by the fresh Sunday morning experience. So if we take Sunday dinner in a restaurant it will be a very special, distinctive place characterized by an emotional environment conducive to the continuation of the worship experience. "The rain that has fallen must be given a chance to soak in the soil." The restaurant must be quiet, with cloth napkins, soft voices, and gentle sounds, so the mood of the morning should not be rudely interrupted before the tranquillizing experience has a chance to seep to the deepest levels and farthest corners of the mind.

Since it is very difficult to control the emotional environment outside of our home we seldom "eat out" on Sundays—but retreat to our home. Here is a distinctive Sunday meal. It is an event! The experience continues. We share our religious faith and feelings at the table. The children are not permitted to go out and play on the streets today. This is a different day. This is a distinctive day. It is God's day. It is the family's day.

No single value has been given a higher priority in our family the past twenty-five years, so our children were never permitted to take jobs which would make them violate this Quiet Zone in Time. With this precept I would never compromise.

Pressures, I know, are enormous and powerful but I urge you for the sake of your spiritual and physical health to carve out a twenty-four-hour Quiet Zone and hold it for a treatment you desperately need.

Dr. Arthur Comstock, researcher, has revealed that "regular churchgoers have fewer heart attacks." Of course.

There is a hymn often sung in church that says it well:

> O day of Rest and Gladness
> O day of Joy and Light
> O balm of Care and Sadness,
> Most Beautiful and Bright!

> Peace be with you!